DIFFICULT LIVES

HITCHING RIDES

DIFFICULT LIVES
HITCHING RIDES

JAMES SALLIS

SYNDICATE BOOKS
NEW YORK

This volume published in 2024 by Syndicate Books

www.syndicatebooks.com

Distributed by
Soho Press, Inc.
227 W 17th Street
New York, NY 10011

Library of Congress Cataloging-in-Publication Data is available

ISBN: 978-1-68199-044-6
eISBN: 978-1-68199-045-3

Cover and interior design by Jeff Wong

Printed in the United States of America

10 9 8 7 6 5 4 3 2 1

Introduction to the New Edition

One looks back on work published over 25 years ago with a mix of parental pride ("Gee, look what the kid could do") and terrible premonition. *Difficult Lives*, which emerged in a series of one-room apartments from a short-story writer in the throes of turning novelist, came about because I'd been reading deeply into the work of these singular writers and, when I looked about for information about them, found little. I began to pull and patch together what I could. The resulting essays appeared in literary journals—High Plains Literary Review, North Dakota Quarterly, Western Humanities Review—and, having decided to hang out on the street corner together, became a book. Published in 1993 by Gary Lovisi at Gryphon Books, it put on fresh clothes for a new edition seven years later and, before joining the perhaps 150 species that fall into extinction daily, was kindly received.

Like my vintage guitars and banjos, these pieces look pretty beat in today's light, but they have a sound all their own. Reading over them, for each time I marvel at having got something just right, soon I founder upon awkward phrasing or blowsy, overblown sentences. Neither are these appreciations simply bits of my personal history; they are as well dots on a line, part of the continuum of criticism theretofore and subsequently afforded these writers. Though little enough was available at the time I wrote, a few sandwiches and salad plates, these days one might feed multitudes from the biographies, commentaries and criticism available. We have two Thompson biographies, innumerable essays, introductions and the like, Garnier's fine new, English-language version of his Goodis book, three biographies now of Himes.

So here's a third edition of *Difficult Lives*. That some material may have been brought into question, become commonplace, even been supplanted by later workers in the field, concerns me little; these essays did their work, which was to knock at doors and windows to urge just such interest in these writers. For this reason I've elected to make no updates incorporating new material and information. Though the Himes essay, for instance, led in time to a fullblown biography, during the writing of which I'd learn so much more, I see no reason to attempt reconstructing my original, less complex, less informed vision of his work; what's written here should be allowed to stand on its own. Thus revisions for this edition have been chiefly editorial, judicious cuts hither and yon, a reshaping of misbegotten phrases or sentences, deletions of some of the repetitions and redundancies of that stuttery younger writer.

Writing has forever been how I find my way to what I truly think. These essays are no exception and, reading them now, distinctly I recall sitting in circles of light in a room outside Dallas or in a two-room upstairs flat in Fort Worth, tapping away at a typewriter with stacks of second-hand paperbacks on the table by me, poking at the seams and innards of these books, trying to puzzle out the clockwork of them, find the muscle, the mystery.

We can't, of course. Each time we think we have it, it shifts and turns in our hands, changes shape, becomes something else. That's the grace and beauty of this weirdness we call art. That's why, as readers, as writers, we go on.

Here again, then, are a few shapes thrown against the wall.

James Sallis
Phoenix
January 2016

TABLE OF CONTENTS

DIFFICULT LIVES

HITCHING RIDES

DIFFICULT
LIVES

Introduction

Many years ago, in temporary self-exile, burrowing under covers with endless cups of tea as hot as I could bear them in my unheated two-room flat off Portobello Road in London, I first read the novels of Hammett and Chandler, all of them, I think, in a single week's time.

My other great passion of the time, equally new, was French literature, and Gide's description of the detective story as a form in which "every character is trying to deceive all the others and in which the truth slowly becomes visible through the haze of deception" seems to me still the finest description both of the appeal these stories have at their deepest level and of the way, confused by sense and memory, confounded by our own and others' notions of things, we actually live our lives.

So as I fed coins into the electric meter and went out each morning for my day's shopping, as my accent gradually fell into cadence with those around me, I came to perceive the detective story as a cornerstone of American literature, another of those quirky American gifts to the world, like blues before, that forever transformed it.

What these stories were about, it seems to me, had little to do with solving any particular crime or restoring moral order. Indeed, crimes were rarely solved—at best, they were understood, just as often were compounded—and much of their power derived from a recognition that there is no moral order save that which a man creates for himself. Like high art, these stories worked hard to unfold the lies society tells us and the lies we tell ourselves. They opened up the clean, well-lit American corpse and dragged its dark heart into sunlight.

Now, commercial literature is not supposed to do that. It's expected to reinforce received wisdom, not challenge it; to reassure us that the perspectives and prejudices we hold are the right ones.

The detective story as Americanized by hardboiled writers had become in fact a fullblown outlaw literature, an extension of the frontier literature embodied in Cooper and Twain. America was symbol and actuality at the same time, ship and sea in one, and uniquely, destructively, we tried to live at both levels. Unable to abide society's false values and order, the American loner—Cooper's Deerslayer, Twain's Huck Finn—moved ever farther from the encroachments of that society, ever farther to the interior, to the west, until, with Chandler's California, there is no more frontier.

In a survey of the genre written in the 1940s, Edmund Wilson noted that the American detective story, unlike its British counterpart, concerns itself not with puzzles and solutions, but with a profound malaise which it conveys to the reader, a sense of conspiracies and corruptions—evil, if you will—surfacing everywhere.

Hammett had invested the myth, relocating demons from European castles and New England settlements to bus stops, diners, rooms in cheap hotels. Chandler in turn had given that new demonology a clear, unmistakable voice.

"Men murdered themselves into this democracy," D.H. Lawrence wrote, and because popular culture is history in caricature, the nation's mind and heart in high relief, the detective story is one abiding record of that democracy, and of that nation.

• • •

I am writing, here, primarily of three novelists: Chester Himes, David Goodis and Jim Thompson. Much of what I say, of course, touches generally upon the American detective story, paperback novels and commercial fiction of the Fifties, the relation of a writer's life to his work. I make no extravagant claims for their work as enduring literature, or few, and am every bit as interested in their failures and incapacities as in their achievements.

Himes, Goodis and Thompson dwell in a peculiar historical cul-de-sac. Certainly I don't deny the importance and impact of their work

(I am, after all, writing about them at book length), but I do claim, as an integral part of my interest, that these books could not have existed at any other time. They are sports in the truest sense, sudden mutations arising in response to specific conditions and failing to continue as a strain once those conditions have passed.

The pulps were far too formulaic to allow much individual expression, subsequent paperbacks too set in form and too overseen, but for a brief period in the latter's early days, when demands were high for new product and no one had really figured out what these books were supposed to be, there were chinks you could drive large typewriters through. Writers who worked within certain minimal guidelines and who could get their pigs to market pretty much on time were otherwise left alone to do much as they wished. Astonishingly, they were able to make a living at this. And writing fast, without the cushion of convention, they reached down and pulled out whatever they found there within themselves, repeating this procedure from book to book so that the best of them turned from simply telling stories to pursuing personal demons, to an exploration of evil and states of mind generally considered the domain of more ambitious literature.

The American genius is at any rate a quirky one, and these are marvelously quirky books. Chester Himes' detective novels mimic traditions of dissembling by which blacks for generations maintained lives parallel to the larger culture; his Harlem is an improvised patchwork of white preconceptions, savagery and absurdist comedy. David Goodis rewrote essentially the same book again and again, ceremonially encoding his own fall from promising writer to recluse. Jim Thompson populated his novels with smiling psychopaths: door-to-door salesmen, con artists, fugitives and deputy sheriffs whose eyes lure the reader towards a great void.

• • •

The pulps in which the hardboiled form originated were truly phenomenal, a great sea of millions upon millions of words out of whose formulaic plots and hackneyed scenes society's true nature surfaced from time to time, like the head of a snake.

Original paperbacks continued, extended, that role. But around the poor seams and creaky joints of some of these books, a heaviness began to settle, while at their hearts gathered an intensity rarely seen in popular literature. "The unoccupied mind feeds on itself," Wallace Stevens wrote. So does the over-occupied—hence these novels, these expeditions to the interior.

American culture has the sad habit of abandoning things it has loved briefly. For too many years Chester Himes' novels remained out of print, for too many years copies of books by Jim Thompson and David Goodis curled and darkened like autumn leaves in basements and attics, molded in old bookstores and thrift shops, propped up the leg of Aunt Peg's card table in the back room. Now, at last, we have found them anew.

Portable Worlds: The Original Paperback Novel

I was six or seven, I guess, when I first began noticing it. It sat for years on one of the end tables, not too far from a framed photograph of General MacArthur, in a living room closed off from the rest of the house except on holidays. No one ever read it, I'm sure. I no longer recall what was depicted on its cover, but I remember it with surprising physicality: the weight of it, that yellowing waxy cover, its smell, the block of urgent words on the back, Complete and Unabridged on its front. It had become an object of mystery to me, an emblem of a world beyond that Fifties house where we never locked doors and doubted no one's values because they were, after all, had to be, the same as ours.

It was, I know now, a Pocket Books reprint of Hammett's *The Glass Key*, a book which would reenter my life some twenty-two years later in a flat off Portobello Road in London where, fortified with immense cups of tea, I read all morning, wrote all afternoon and evening.

Paperbacks had begun their subversive life five years before my own birth, in 1939, with Pocket Books' release of ten trial titles such as *Lost Horizon*, *Wuthering Heights* and *Topper*. Ten thousand copies of each were printed, and the books were to be sold only in New York. With the phenomenal success of paperbacks and their rapid growth as an industry, early praise for Pocket Books' democratic spirit in making literature accessible to the masses changed to cries of scorn and horror at this degradation of mass taste, suggesting that general attitudes were not too terribly different from those which had occasioned an 1898 editorial in *The New York Times* concerning the earliest paperbacks, intended for travelers:

> The torn cover bears the soil of the journey, and even after the story is forgotten, the book yet spells sandwiches, cinders and satchel to tired eyes as long as it lies on the table. In desperation you stick it in the bookcase, but all the world can see that it's a parvenu. The choice vellums draw away from it, the daintily bound essays and poems will have none of it, solemn history frowns on it, polite fiction scorns it, well-fed reference books turn their backs on the waif of the station. Even the recherché travel (its fortune in leather) fails to take pity on this poor "little brother of the rich." Though you put all the paper-covered volumes on a shelf by themselves, the result is not better, for you have incorporated a little slum district in the literary community.

True, it's a long bus ride from Shakespeare to *Swamp Girl*. And the paperbacks took their little ghetto, their slum district, to heart, setting up barricades and launching a direct assault on "polite fiction."

Every culture, every society, has its outlaw literature, its specific vision of life's underside: crocodiles floating half-submerged in supposedly calm waters. Medieval Europe's bawdy farces, Regency England's gothics, Victorian penny dreadfuls, American dime novels and Depression-era pulps all filled this function. In a demotic society such as ours, paperbacks became the breeding ground and natural home for a demotic literature. Parenthetically it's of interest to note that the democratization of evil (Hammett's relocation of it to the urban, quotidian scene), that of style (the Black Mask writers) and that of literature itself (the paperback book) occurred more or less simultaneously.

From the first, paperbacks embraced their subversive role. In his remarkable tribute to them, *Hardboiled America: The Lurid Years of Paperbacks*, Geoffrey O'Brien writes: "These novels, and the covers that illustrate them, speak of the ignoble corners of life beyond the glow of Jane Powell, Father Knows Best, and the healthy, smiling faces in magazines advertising milk or frozen dinners or trips to California."

Even the cool, cynical tough-guy tone adopted by most of these books was an antidote to American bombast and self-touting. That tone, coupled with sharp dialog, gave hardboiled fiction a double-impact immediacy that instantly hooked the reader and ultimately found purchase in the greater culture. David Madden argues:

> Events and conditions of the Twenties and Thirties were a cause that produced the Hammett "Black Mask" kind of detective and they in turn were the cause of certain attitudes that produced behaviour in the Twenties and Thirties. [These stories] provided not only escape from conditions but criticism of those conditions as well. They provided simultaneously American dreams and American nightmares.

Madden implies here that this fiction, this genre, actually changed our perception of the world, giving us new templates for our lives, a new, twentieth-century, urban mythology. Our enduring fascination with hardboiled stories and their immediacy of voice, with the subterfuge and subterranean suspensions of guilt at their heart—this, and particularly the recent resurgence of noir fiction—bear him out.

Fifties paperbacks, O'Brien writes, likewise were a microcosm of American fantasies about the real world, investing ordinary streets, dives, tenements and cheap hotels with mystery, with a kind of obdurate poetry. Popular culture, after all is history in caricature; these books are thimble-size monuments, frozen sections of our culture's history, "the dream America made of itself, a few decades ago" and the nightmares welling up beneath. If we look hard (O'Brien goes on) we can still discern in these tiny figures the heroes and demons of a generation, the archetypes of an era haunted by unspeakable violence and tormented by desires it cannot fulfill.

> Shamelessly exploitative, they made their points with a maximum of directness. No trace of subtlety was permitted to cloud the violent and erotic visions that were their essence, and that very lack of subtlety lifted them out of this world.

Tawdry—with just a hint of transcendence.

· · ·

The style of our own time, when we look back years from now, may well be like something from MTV, mannerist, hard-edged and a bit surreal, wildly eclectic: iconic images that seem to have no center, no meaning. Pound was right, every age demands its image; and the Fifties are those paperback covers—"flat, bright, violent surfaces devoid of character but brimming with emotion"—posted like warnings at the threshold: Enter At Your Own Risk, Abandon Pretense All Who Enter Here, No Serious Readers Allowed.

Mysteries in 1945 comprised half of all paperbacks published. By 1950 this figure was down to 26%, 13% by 1955. A new beast had come about and now slouched towards the drugstores, sidewalk news stands and truck stops of America. Ephemeral as the newspapers and candy wrappers in whose shadow it sprouted, it was not a mystery in any traditional sense yet came spring-loaded with action, awash with violence and illicit (if mostly implied) sex.

Harry Whittington in 1948 had quit his government job of sixteen years and, leaping in "fully clothed, where only fools treaded water," set up as a writer.

> At that precise moment, the publishing world was being turned upside down by the Fawcett Publishing Company. When they lost a huge reprint paperback distribution client, they decided to do the unheard of, the insane. They published original novels at 25 cents a copy. Print order on each title: 250,000. They paid writers not by royalty but on print order. Foreign, movie and TV rights remained with the writer. They were insane. They were my kind of people.

Once called "king of the paperback pioneers," Whittington published dozens of novels in all categories, stark westerns, tightly plotted action-suspense stories, unrelievedly noir fiction—edge literature, all of it. Like others such as David Goodis, suddenly he found it possible to sustain himself writing more or less what he wished, producing a body of work unified by its author's preoccupations and instinctive feints. He had wanted to be the next Fitzgerald but after writing a mystery story on Monday, mailing it in on Tuesday, and receiving a check for $250 on Friday, switched horses. For better than two decades Whittington sold every word he wrote; at one point he contracted to provide a 60,000-word novel each month for over three years.

> It all seemed so great at the time: Doing what I wanted to do, living as I wanted to live, having the time of my life and

being paid for it. I worked hard; nobody ever wrote and sold 150-odd novels in twenty years without working hard, but I loved what I was doing.

Cornell Woolrich is another writer who early dreamed of becoming the new Fitzgerald, and who remains a kind of exemplar of the paperback novelist. Initial promise and success with chronicles of the Jazz Age such as *Cover Charge* (1926) and *Children of the Ritz* (1927) were followed by a long decline: failure at Hollywood scriptwriting, an ill-fated brief marriage, alcoholism, self-imprisonment in cheap hotel rooms and the ruins of his memory. Yet finding in the mid-Thirties, in mystery publications like Black Mask and Dime Detective, a voice for his own loneliness, fear and despair—a container he thought might hold them—Woolrich went on to turn out a dozen novels, several of them remaining continuously in print, and well over 200 stories and novellas, one of which provided the source for Hitchcock's Rear Window.

Michael Avallone's thumbnail biography of Woolrich could easily be a description of one of Goodis' or Thompson's characters, and oddly synopsizes the world of the paperback novel:

> [He] lived some forty years of his lifetime in a hotel room; he had no close personal friends and the Big Romance always eluded him; some of his most memorable works are dedicated to such lifeless things as hotel rooms, typewriters and the utter sadness of the human condition; later on in life he discovered John Barleycorn and the empty days and nights of his withdrawal from society echoed and re-echoed with the typical alcoholic miseria of broken appointments, paranoiac harangues and self-lashing which ended in the usual weeping haze of Where did I go wrong?

Paranoia is, in fact, Woolrich's theme and fundamental plot. His characters cling to the fringes of life—living in seedy hotels, eating at greasy spoons, looking for companionship in dancehalls—and horrible things happen to them.

His plots often are wildly implausible, but Woolrich depicts his characters, and the sorry states in which they find themselves, with painful vividness; this exactness of description dramatically intensifies the prevailing sense of impotence and doom.

Film critic Michael Price once suggested that the then-current resurgence of film noir was a kind of dialectic, surfacing, it seems abruptly, in response to what was actually a decade-long opposition between the dark visions of filmmakers such as Ridley Scott and "film lite" movies by Lucas, Spielberg et fils. Film lite, Price said, offers fables decked out in their parents' clothes, pats on the back telling you it's all going to be all right. Film noir tells you that nothing is going to be all right, ever; that individual will is illusion, helplessness the eternal human condition; that we are broken by the beasts caged within us as surely as by terrible forces (corporations, conspiracies) without.

Woolrich's tales of despair and impotence struck a similar tone and accord with readers of the Forties, which O'Brien calls the era of "the Great Fear," doing what popular art at its best does best: limning shifts in a culture's course before the culture itself begins to perceive those shifts, pulling out of the collective mind a few signal images to leave behind on the walls— stylized, totemic—as a record of those who once lived here.

• • •

Paperbacks were orphans, half-breeds, barnyard animals air-dropped into displays of exotic fauna, turkeys that had learned to swim, fish that could almost fly. No one knew quite what to do with them, least of all the people who were producing them and who tended to be a mixed lot themselves: burned-out bookmen, immigrants from food and other wholesale distribution, nickel-hearted entrepreneurs, renegade intellectuals.

The early paperback industry, then, was a loose, improvisational affair, operating under conditions anarchic enough to allow unexpected and remarkable freedoms—and because of those freedoms, some of the most idiosyncratic and intense work in American literature.

O'Brien writes of the cracks that writers like Jim Thompson and David Goodis fell through in the "ramshackle industry" of early paperbacks:

> Amid all the mechanical duplication of iconography, a few
> writers recorded their own visions. The work of these few remains
> readable to the extent that they made their own variations on
> the public myth, variations not often noticed in a market equally

receptive to the well-worn. These writers make up a strange and melancholy collection of individuals—melancholy at least in part because of the sense of dissatisfaction with their own work that so often emerges. That dissatisfaction, shared by Hammett and Chandler, seems to haunt the hardboiled genre, in contract to the verve and toughness of the foreground. The great American nightmare of Failure is never far off.

What we have here, then, are three writers who thought like Icarus to fly but fell into a sea of original paperback novels. Three highly individual voices almost lost to the babble and hubbub of the marketplace. Three men who tried in their work to subvert again an already subversive genre and simultaneously to retrieve their lives, make some sense of them, through parlor tricks of metaphor.

All three collided with limitations of the form and with limitations within themselves, and fell—fell as we all fall, as we go on all our lives learning how to fall, hoping to achieve some measure of grace in the act.

There's a poem by W.S. Merwin, "Fly," that I always read to students in writing classes. Merwin describes his attempts to teach a fat, good-natured old pigeon to fly, throwing the scruffy, trusting bird again and again into the air demanding that it fly until one day he finds the pigeon in the dovecote, "dead of the needless efforts."

> So that is what I am
>
> Pondering his eye that could not
> Conceive that I was a creature to run from
>
> I who have always believed too much in words

Here are three men who, in their particular ways, at a particular time in the history of our nation, believed too much in words.

Jim Thompson: Dime-Store Dostoevski

"Nobody else ever wrote books like these," Barry Gifford says of him.

When Jim Thompson died in 1977 at age 70 after more than fifty years' work as a professional writer, every one of his 29 novels was out of print.

Disposability, of course, was a given: Thompson wrote paperback novels, candy wrapper books that supplanted the pre-war throwaway pulps and prefigured, then briefly paralleled, B movies and ephemeral TV. These books were jobbed out to distributors who lugged them by the carton to bus depots, drugstores and the like and offloaded them onto wire racks studded with colorful tin badges bearing the various publishers' logos; once read, like beer cans they were tossed away.

In one four-year period in the Fifties Thompson produced thirteen novels while co-writing, with Stanley Kubrick, that director's first feature film, *The Killing*. By the Sixties the paperback original was largely a thing of the past, and so, it seemed, sadly, was Jim Thompson; in the last years of his life he began and abandoned over a dozen novels, working up portion after portion for his agents then, with no interest from publishers forthcoming, moving on to yet another.

Only in France, where Thompson's books remained more or less continuously in print and received an acclaim similar to that given Hammett, McCoy, Cain and other major roman noir writers, did Thompson's work endure. A handful of American writers and readers remembered that work with a mixture of fondness and awe: its starkness, its savage, unrelenting voice and emotional contortions. One of those was poet, novelist, biographer and part-time publisher Barry Gifford, who on a trip to Paris came across a batch of Thompson novels in a bookstore bin and recalled reading, at age 12, *The Killer Inside Me*. Returning to the States with a sackful of French editions, he began seeking out surviving copies of the originals and, in 1984, under the Black Lizard imprint, brought out new editions of four Jim Thompson novels in garish, waxy covers reminiscent of the original ones. Nine further Thompson titles followed from Black Lizard, along with similar work by David Goodis, Harry Whittington, Frederic Brown and others. Donald I. Fine responded to growing interest in Thompson's work with two novel collections and with *Fireworks*, an anthology of "lost writings" spanning sixty years. More recently Vintage Books, assuming Black Lizard's catalog, has brought out many of Thompson's novels in uniform editions, along with cognate work of Himes, Goodis, Whittington and others.

"At the outermost edge of American literature, in a swamp previously inhabited only by Hubert Selby and William Burroughs, Jim Thompson awaits reclamation," wrote the editors of that anthology, Robert Polito and Michael McCauley. "Buried under the shabbiest conventions of pulp fiction—all but three of the 29 books he published between 1942 and 1973 were paperback originals—and picking at the banality with offhand brilliance, his novels pursue the most debased imaginative materials. Reading one of them is like being trapped in a bomb shelter with a chatty maniac who also happens to be the air raid warden."

Now, it seems, the salvage is well underway. The swamp's being dredged daily for bodies, and they come up out of it in pieces, corrupt and at the same time somehow simpler, purer, staring at us with a fixed, terrible regard: the novels of Jim Thompson.

• • •

I killed Amy Stanton on Saturday night on the fifth of April, 1952, at a few minutes before nine o'clock.

That's from *The Killer Inside Me*, not from the book's beginning as you might think, but from nearer its end, the eighteenth of twenty-six chapters, much of the novel's narrative having spiraled down to that single, damning action within which the narrator finds a freedom he's never before known. And here, following a chapter of backpedaling and seeming asides, is the actual murder:

And I hit her in the guts as hard as I could.

My fist went back against her spine, and the flesh closed around it to the wrist. I jerked back on it, I had to jerk, and she flopped forward from the waist, like she was hinged.

Her hat fell off, and her head went clear down and touched the floor. And then she toppled over, completely over, like a kid turning a somersault. She lay on her back, eyes bulging, rolling her head from side to side.

She was wearing a white blouse and a light cream-colored suit; a new one, I reckon, because I didn't remember seeing it before. I got my hand in the front of the blouse, and ripped it down to the waist. I jerked the skirt up over her head, and she jerked and shook all over; and there was a funny sound like she was trying to laugh.

And then I saw the puddle spreading out under her.

I sat down and tried to read the paper. I tried to keep my eyes on it. But the light wasn't very good, not good enough to read by, and she kept moving around. It looked like she couldn't lie still.

Once I felt something touch my boot, and I looked down and it was her hand. It was moving back and forth across the toe of my boot. It moved up along the ankle and the leg, and somehow I was afraid to move away. And then her fingers were at the top, clutching down inside; and I almost couldn't move. I stood up and tried to jerk away, and the fingers held on.

I dragged her two-three feet before I could break away.

That's vintage, distilled Thompson. Starting out as standard pulp violence, suddenly it becomes something else, something reptilian, the narrator's apartness and near-paralysis underscored by precisions of description and by the claustrophobic feel of the whole thing, discontinuities of thought and action (that disembodied hand, serial use of the word *jerk*) coupled with chant-like repetitions and those unrelenting *ands*.

The Killer Inside Me, with its psychopathic deputy sheriff, is generally acknowledged as Thompson's masterpiece. Its one clear contender, in many ways a twin, is *Pop. 1280*, a marvelously sustained comedy. Both novels have been filmed—the second brilliantly, transplanted to French West Africa, by Bertrand Tavernier as Coup de Torchon—but Thompson's distinctive voice is what makes these books, and the discrete vocabulary of film relinquishes much of that.

Pop. 1280's first-person narrator, like *Killer*'s Lou Ford a lawman, sheriffs over a godforsaken, retrograde plot of land called Pottsville, "twelve hundred and eighty souls" bunched together and lost in the wastes of West Texas. Every bit as bleak as that of *Killer*, the book's dark vision comes wrapped in the swaddling clothes and dissembling monologue (monotone, as well) of Nick Corey's interior life, at the apex of a demotic comic tradition reaching back through Twain to Bierce and Artemus Ward. Here is Pottsville's ordained savior, introducing himself in the first of twenty-four chapters:

Well, sir, I should have been sitting pretty, just about as pretty as a man could sit. Here I was, the high sheriff of Potts County, and I was drawing almost two thousand a year—not to mention what I could pick up on the side. On top of that, I had free living quarters on the second floor of the courthouse, just as nice a place as a man could ask for; and it even had a bathroom so that I didn't have to bathe in a washtub or tramp outside to a privy, like most folks in town did. I guess you could say that Kingdom Come was really here as far as I was concerned. I had it made—being high sheriff of Potts County—as long as I minded my own business and didn't arrest no one unless I just couldn't get out of it and they didn't amount to nothin'.

And yet I was worried. I had so many troubles that I was worried plumb sick.

I'd sit down to a meal of maybe half a dozen pork chops and a few fried eggs and a pan of hot biscuits with grits and gravy, and I couldn't eat it. Not all of it. I'd start worrying about those problems of mine, and the next thing you knew I was getting up from the table with food still left on my plate.

It was the same way with sleeping. You might say I didn't really get no sleep at all. I'd climb in bed, thinking this was one night I was bound to sleep, but I wouldn't. It'd be maybe twenty or thirty minutes before I could doze off. And then, no more than eight or nine hours later, I'd wake up. Wide awake. And I couldn't go back to sleep, frazzled and wore out as I was.

Well, sir, I was layin' awake like that one night, tossing and turning and going plumb out of my mind, until finally I couldn't stand it no longer. So I says to myself, "Nick," I says, "Nick Corey, these problems of yours are driving you plumb out of your mind, so you better think of something fast. You better come to a decision, Nick Corey, or you're gonna wish you had."

So I thought and I thought, and then I thought some more. And finally I came to a decision.

I decided I didn't know what the heck to do.

By book's end, of course, he's more or less decided that he does know, like Miss Lonelyhearts (and with equally disastrous consequences) taking on responsibility for the world, or at least for Pottsville: "why else had I been put here in Potts County, and why else did I stay here? Why else, who else, what else but Christ Almighty would put up with it?"

Now it is quite unsettling to open the pages of a cheap paperback novel and find yourself staring into Satan's calm face, or Christ's troubled one. Genre conventions themselves are supposed to protect you, holding forth a world parallel to your own but sealed off from it and, whatever the wrath and wreckage, somehow safe. But Jim Thompson's work is one long assault on the words *supposed to*, and Thompson rarely submitted to the plot formulas editors expected. In fact, he methodically destroys those clichés—not by transcending them as a more "literary" writer might, but by sinking so thoroughly, so unremittingly into them that they're stood on their heads. Finally, as Polito and McCauley note, Thompson's "nods to hard-boiled conventions do not so much toughen Thompson's novels as humanize them—they're all we have to hang onto in the ferocious downdraft."

R.V. Cassill, in his fine appreciation of *The Killer Inside Me*, makes much the same point. Democratic man, he writes, uses the fiction of violence for its purgative effect but does not want to be purged forcefully. At every level we find "novels of protest and violence affirming the indissoluble contiguity of the democratic mass, the adequacy of received ideas, and the justice of our aspirations towards a Better World," and the writer who chooses crime and violence as his theme yet wishes to go beyond neutralizing conventions may be setting himself quite apart from his readers.

Certainly Thompson's refusal to play by rules and his dark vision condemned him to the ghetto of original-paperback publication, thereby assuring the anonymity and critical disregard that eventually helped stifle his voice. (Gagged by the silence of others, in Sartre's phrase.) But just as certainly, original-paperback publication allowed him what otherwise could not have been possible: this let him go on writing, let him go on pushing at the borders of a world uniquely his.

"Jim Thompson breaks most of the rules of crime fiction, or indeed any kind of genre fiction," Geoffrey O'Brien points out in his afterword for the Black Lizard reprints. "With his drawling raconteur's voice, his beautifully modulated story-telling rhythms, and his endless stock of anecdote and naturalistic color, he sets us up for a sucker punch in which the bottom drops out of everything: location, narrative, personality itself."

That perception seems to me central to understanding Jim Thompson's work. Beginning with the subversion of genre conventions and clichés, slowly and insidiously Thompson progresses to a subversion of character and, finally, of existence itself. One thinks of those cartoon beasts who, going about their destined business, pause to look down and only then discover that the ground beneath their feet—for how long?—no longer exists. But in Thompson's work there is no restoration. The following frames show the coyote still scorched and smoldering, stripped of hide and hair, foreshortened, legless, transformed.

Again and again, in whatever formulation, this basic truth struggles to light in commentary on Thompson's work: "We are always on the edge," "undercutting any sense of stability to get to the heart of his nightmare," "There's no point of goodness in his books to refer to."

Relentless, unregenerative, beyond redemption: the world of Jim Thompson. Sexuality is synonymous with violence, sometimes implicit, more often manifest; grotesque marriages begin in alcoholism and flight and end in murder; driven, characters circle and stalk one another without quite knowing why. Rarely has an American writer, a resolutely commercial writer at that, given forth so bleak and damning a vision. One drops his dime into the peek-show nickelodeon and, fitting eyes to viewpiece, finds himself peering into the abyss.

I found a long hair sticking out of my nose, and I jerked it out and looked at it, and it didn't look particularly interesting. I dropped it to the floor, wonderin' if falling hair from fella's noses was noted along with fallin' sparrows. I raised up on one cheek of my butt, and eased out one of those long rattly farts, like you never can get rid of when other folks are around.

That numb, dull stare into the void, and that voice, are Jim Thompson. Whatever the felicities of setting—small-town sheriffing, life as an itinerant salesman, the daily grit and grind of journalism—all along, in a kind of furious subterfuge, that voice is chipping away at the very reality the story carefully constructs, talking about the story's people and events, draining them slowly of motive and emotion until only the voice itself remains. In many ways *Savage Night*'s protagonist is an exemplar for all Thompson's protagonists: "The darkness and myself. Everything else was gone. And the little that was left of me was going, faster and faster."

What are we to make, finally, of these recurrent themes and preoccupations? Certainly, like Goodis, Woolrich and others of his time, to some extent Jim Thompson began writing in order to confront personal demons; and once given provisional form those demons, as they will, grew ever more substantial. But the world view of the novels, their summary vision, suggests a coherence quite beyond that, as perceived by Cassill in his argument that Thompson is in effect breaking the back of the genre to write a novel of ideas. In novel after novel, for all their temporal disparity, for all the intricacies of background and the distinctiveness of protagonists, we confront the same godless, dissolving world.

Geoffrey O'Brien, with no sense of patronage, calls Thompson a dime-store Dostoevski, and goes on to say:

> The temptation is to read his books simply as testimonials of his own compulsions. Indeed, the recurrence of certain images—the murderous mother, the helpless father, the termagant wife, the terminally alienated, often impotent husband—invites such a reading. Yet although Thompson's specific obsessions are personal, their tone belongs to the culture at large. His plot materials derive from the atrocities of the daily papers—he was, after all, a reporter and a regular contributor to True Detective—and his settings distill a lifetime's worth of highways and railroad yards and hotel lobbies. It's all too clear that, far from being subjective fantasies,

Thompson's books faithfully reflect a mentality that seethes all around us, as American as the next mass murder.

Perhaps Thompson's greatest gift is for luring the reader into the cave of his protagonist-narrator's consciousness. Forever aware that the horrors of the individual psyche are rooted in formal horrors of state, church and family, one ear homing always towards "the terrible voice of justification," Thompson brings the reader to identify with his monsters, brings us almost to sympathy with their helplessness and mangled innocence. The quiet monologue of madness goes on and on, at times uncertain just what story it's telling, other times lying outright, irredeemably amused at humankind, sweeping us along like a tour guide past dreadful shoals and unimaginable cataclysms as though they're the most natural things in the world.

• • •

The Killer Inside Me, published in 1952, was Jim Thompson's fourth book, and the first of his paperback originals. He was already a prolific contributor to trade journals, pulps and true-crime magazines. *Now and On Earth* had appeared in 1942, supposedly written in ten days on a typewriter, and in a hotel room, supplied by its publisher; *Heed the Thunder* came out four years later. *Nothing More Than Murder* (1949) was his first crime novel, written at age 43 in a clash with desperate finances, and it contains many of the elements we now recognize as Thompson signatures: murderous protagonist ensconced within a stream of glib patter, tangle of twisted sexual relationships, elaborately detailed background of some hinterland of human enterprise (in this case, the film distribution business).

Despite apocrypha that *Killer* was written to order to a plot given him by editor Arnold Hano at Lion Books, Thompson seems to have carried in mind for some years the basic configuration of the novel. In his fanciful autobiography *Bad Boy* (1953), Thompson writes of a laconic deputy sheriff who came to collect a fine where he was working oil rigs outside Big Spring, Texas.

I stared down at him. Finally, I found my voice. "Have a nice ride?"
"Tol'able. Left town last night."

"Well, here I am," I said. "Come on and get me."

"Ain't in no hurry. Just as soon rest a spell."

"Why don't you shoot me?" I said. "I'm a pretty desperate criminal."

"Ain't got no gun." He grinned up at me lazily. "Never seen much sense in shooting. And that's a fact."

He stretched out on the derrick floor and put his hands under his head. He closed his eyes.

I sat on a crosspiece for a while, smoking. Then I climbed up to the top of the rig and took a hatchet from my belt. I chopped at the edge of the crown block, sending down a shower of grease-soaked splinters.

He brushed them off, lazily, pulling his hat over his face.

I chopped out a small piece of the block, catching it in my hand before it could fall. I took careful aim and let go.

It struck near the side of his head, bounced into the air and landed between his folded hands. He sat up. He looked up at me, then looked at the piece of wood. He took out his pocketknife and began to whittle.

. . .

He was a good-looking guy. His hair was coal-black beneath his pushed-back Stetson, and his black intelligent eyes were set wide apart in a tanned, fine-featured face. He grinned at me as I dropped down in front of him on the derrick floor.

"Now, that wasn't very smart," he said. "And that's—"

"And that's a fact," I snapped. "All right, let's get going."

He went on grinning at me. In fact, his grin broadened a little. But it was fixed, humorless, and a veil seemed to drop over his eyes.

"What makes you so sure," He said, softly, "you're going anywhere?"

"Well, I—" I gulped. "I—I—"

"Awful lonesome out here, ain't it? Ain't another soul for miles around but you and me."

"L-look," I said. "I'm—I wasn't trying to—"

"Lived here all my life," he went on, softly. "Everyone knows me. No one know you. And we're all alone. What you make o' that, a smart fella like you? You've been around. You're all full of piss and high spirits. What do you think an ol' stupid country boy might do in a case like this?"

23

He stared at me, steadily, the grin baring his teeth. I stood paralyzed and wordless, a great cold lump forming in my stomach. The wind whined and moaned through the derrick. He spoke again, as though in answer to a point I had raised.

"Don't need one," he said. "Ain't nothin' you can do with a gun that you can't do a better way. Don't see nothin' around here I'd need a gun for."

He shifted his feet slightly. The muscles in his shoulders bunched. He took a pair of black kid gloves from his pocket, and drew them on, slowly. He smacked his fist into the palm of his other hand.

"I'll tell you something," he said. "Tell you a couple of things. There ain't no way of telling what a man is by looking at him. There ain't no way of knowing what he'll do if he has the chance. You think maybe you can remember that?"

I couldn't speak, but I managed a nod. His grin and his eyes went back to normal.

"Look kind of peaked," he said. "Why'n't you have somethin' to eat an' drink before we leave?"

...

I never saw that deputy again, but I couldn't get him out of my mind. And the longer he remained there the bigger riddle he presented.

Again and again Thompson tried to get the deputy down on paper, that meld of menace and dispassion, but while it was all so real to him, he couldn't make it *seem* real. To do that, he had to get outside his own head and into the deputy's.

Finally, as I matured, I was able to recreate him on paper— the sardonic, likeable murderer of my fourth novel, *The Killer Inside Me*. But I was a long time in doing it—almost thirty years.

And I still haven't got him out of my mind.

• • •

Besides *The Killer Inside Me*, 1952 saw publication of Thompson's *Cropper's Cabin*, Ross Macdonald's *The Ivory Grin*, David Goodis'

24

Of Tender Sin and *Street of the Lost,* Mickey Spillane's *Kiss Me, Deadly.* The year before had brought a Goodis classic, *Cassidy's Girl,* Macdonald's *The Way Some People Die,* three Spillanes, and books by Cornell Woolrich and Kenneth Fearing. The following year was something of a watershed: three Goodis novels, William Burrough's *Junkie,* Chandler's *The Long Goodbye,* and five from Thompson: *The Criminal, Bad Boy, The Alcoholics, Savage Night,* and *Recoil.*

Nineteen-fifty-two also brought the paperback industry under investigation by the House Select Committee on Current Pornographic Materials, determined, as O'Brien remarks, to make the world safe for the Saturday Evening Post. And that remark is apt, for very likely it was not specifically sexual content to which the Committee objected so much as it was the whole air of subversion endemic to paperback activity: "These novels, and the covers that illustrate them, speak of the ignoble corners of life beyond the glow of Jane Powell, Father Knows Best, and the healthy, smiling faces in magazines advertising milk or frozen dinners or trips to California," great garish raspberries blown in the face of the American myth.

These books deal with the hard edge of things—the jagged seam of buildings against a city sky, the sudden thrust of a billboard or an oil rig or violence—and in this literalness, this paring-down, finally attain a kind of hyperrealism. Of bedraggled hotels, street corner cafes and neon-lit bar rooms these books helped compose a counter-myth still very much at America's heart, investing such cul de sacs of the American dream with a broody, abiding mystery, a kind of poetry.

"The mind makes gods and demons out of the materials at hand," O'Brien notes. "America, the ultimate secular society, could not prevent the inanimate man-made trappings of its life from assuming nightmarish proportions. The dreamer whose heaven is full of things suffers the fate of the fairy-tale character whose wish, too well fulfilled, shatters him. Sex and money, the only objects of desire, lure the individual into places of archaic horror, where monstrous transformations occur. Desire, enraged that it cannot be fulfilled, that the promise was false, turns desperate, paranoid, violent. It destroys what it cannot possess, what it could never have possessed."

And as I write these words, at six A.M. on Thanksgiving Day, 1988, that's still the news, the only news that matters, the heart of it all, for all of us here in America's long shadow.

• • •

By whatever fitful slants or seepage, fiction both reveals and conceals its author. And when in book after book, as with Thompson and Goodis, we encounter identical characters, settings and concerns, rather as though the work pursues some internal logic or dialogue of its own, inevitaby we arrive at questions of congruence between life and writing.

Two biographies now have given us cornerstones for serious study of Jim Thompson. Michael McCauley's *Sleep With the Devil* (1991) is the less formal of the two, concentrating for the greater part on the fiction itself. Robert Polito's award-winning *Savage Art* (1995) offers up a no-holds-barred probing into the wellsprings of Thompson's character and art.

In his introduction McCauley underscores Thompson's essential Manichaeism, one of many threads he attempts to follow back into the maze.

> In his first two novels, Thompson's characters, doomed by heredity and circumstance, fight their fates in an effort to recover a lost world or discover a lost part of their selves; later protagonists are so unsure of their worlds and their selves that there seems nothing left to recover. Thompson was always writing about the same basic condition, whether on a macro or a micro scale: unknowable dualities and unbridgeable gaps— false and true, illusion and reality, good and evil, conscious and unconscious, cause and effect.

Throughout, McCauley never loses sight of the fact that Thompson's work, however cryptic or enciphered, is intended still as communication: urgent semaphore. And its ultimate warning, he insists, is that the self-deceit and confusion of Jim Thompson's murderous psychotics only echo the deceit and confusion inherent in a society more engaged with image, with how things appear, than with actuality.

McCauley's difficulties in writing his book might form the syllabus for a course titled Problems in Biography. He's up against something more than the usual obscurities and silences of time. For as is true of many creative people, both in daily discourse and in his work Jim Thompson continually reinvented himself. Supposed intimations to friends, editors and acquaintances upon investigation turn out to be as hyperbolic, as fictive, as the fanciful novel-autobiographies *Bad Boy* and *Roughneck*. (*Now and On Earth* may be the exception, portraying work in San Diego aircraft factories and Thompson's early family life with what seems reasonable verisimilitude.)

Polito points out that, while the detective novel begins in chaos and ends in a tidied room, momentos neatly set out on shelves, the crime novel, the sort of novel Thompson wrote, begins with chaos held at bare abeyance and, as controls break down, spins ever further out of ken and keep. Polito quotes the protagonist from *Savage Night*:

> You can do that, split yourself up into two parts. It's easier than you think. Where it gets tough is when you try to put the parts back together again.

Parts, small parts, are what we have of Jim Thompson. The life of a freelance writer virtually by definition is isolate. We're alone for years in rooms, scribbling; we're forever a step or two off to the side, looking on. Statements from those who knew him professionally are often so simplistic as to suggest that they in fact knew him hardly at all. He seems to have been always the artful dodger, and often to have taken refuge in the flamboyance and tawdry romanticism riding piggyback on the popular image of the pulp writer.

The family, moreover, has its own Jim Thompson, a quiet, hardworking man, and it guards that image carefully. Mike McCauley remarks the extent to which the family perceives Jim Thompson as townspeople perceive kindly, harmless ol' Lou Ford of *The Killer Inside Me*. One envisions Thompson day after day removing himself from that safe harbor, shutting the door to his workroom, throwing open the screenless backdoors and emergency exits his private world happens behind. It's much the same for the reader who steps into the apparent safety of one of his books and suddenly, one foot raised and about to fall, finds the ground opening beneath.

Finally, there is Jim Thompson's alcoholism, about which he wrote with some distance in *Bad Boy* and *Roughneck*, and with considerable intimacy in his essay "An Alcoholic Looks at Himself," published in

Saga during his tenure as editor there. More of this later, but for now, from that essay:

> An alcoholic, in the unarrested state of his disease, is incapable of sustained effort. He will perform some surprising feat of industry and intelligence, accomplishing, perhaps, six months' work in one. That probably will be all an employer will get out of him, however, for six months plus, provided he stays around that long. For he is not building a future in a job. He is only proving to himself that he can, "if he takes a notion," outwork and out-think any top-notch employee. He is, in short, only justifying his past drinking and establishing his right to continue it.

Illusionist Howard Thurston once advised an assistant: If you don't know what's going on, boy, smile and point the other way. It seems to me that Jim Thompson's revelation of character, the deflection of elements of his own life into fiction, the slow unfolding of his world in book after book—in short, his particular genius—proceeds by much the same feint and misdirection.

Nor does it escape me, sitting here in Fort Worth, a city his early life perpetually circled, cut off just as he was by late nights and early mornings alone at the desk, by these perishable pages and my own disabilities, that in one sense at least I am setting myself in competition with Jim Thompson. For chiefly by force of intuition I am attempting to open the same doors into Jim Thompson's mind and cloistered world that, book after book, he opened into those of the Joe Wilmots, Nick Coreys and Lou Fords of our world.

• • •

Here, briefly, is what we think we know about Jim Thompson.

He was born James Myers Thompson in Anadarko, Oklahoma, in 1907 and grew up in that region, in rural Texas, and in Fort Worth, locations for much of his fiction. His father was a sheriff, de facto lawyer and wildcat oilman who struck it big then lost everything, a restless, unappeased man, and from early days Jim Thompson knew both wealth and poverty, shuttling from boom town to backwoods, to various relatives' homes, to temporary houses and crowded rooms. *Cropper's Cabin*, set in eastern Oklahoma, makes much use of that childhood environment; *Bad Boy* details the family's divagations.

Like so many of his characters unable to fit themselves into the social order, Thompson fared poorly at school, often in trouble, more often absent, finally graduating (just before a breakdown and hospitalization for tuberculosis and alcoholism) only after bribing a fellow schoolmate making out grade reports. For at least the six years of his high-school career, and for some years following, he worked at a staggering variety of jobs: golf caddy, roustabout, actor, newspaperman, bill collector, truck driver, oilfield and pipeline and harvest hand, gambler, con man, steeplejack, bellboy. With publication of his second novel in 1946 he remarked, "I've never wanted to do anything but write for as far back as I can remember, and most of the time I've managed just about anything else."

Thompson married in 1930, and by that time had become rather a prolific contributor to regional publications such as Texas Monthly and Prairie Schooner, to true-crime magazines like True Detective (an interest in crime reportage remained with him throughout his life), and to various trade journals and pulp-fiction magazines. He worked also, peripatetically (as he did everything else), at a number of newspapers including the New York Daily News and L.A. Times-Mirror. Late in that decade he became director of the Federal Writers' Project for Oklahoma; two short stories from this period appear in *Fireworks*.

Thompson wrote his first novel in 1941 following dismissal from a high editorial post and stints as successful freelancer and San Diego aircraft-factory worker. By his own account (certainly hyperbolic, but to what degree is difficult to discern) he packed wife and children off to her parents "for a week or two" and embarked by bus to New York. There, broke, bereft and hung-over, he decided he would extricate himself by writing a novel and began canvassing editorial offices.

> The editor whose office I was admitted to listened to me incredulously, burst into laughter and summarily took me in to see the publisher. That gentleman heard me out, a frown of wonder creasing his forehead.

"Let's see," he said at last. "You want us to ransom you out of your hotel. Then—"

"It's only a few dollars."

"Then you want us to lend you a typewriter and stake you while you're writing a novel, a novel which you don't have very clearly in mind yourself."

"I've got it clear enough. I talk a bad story," I said, "and you only need to stake me for two weeks. You can't lose very much. When I turn in the novel you can hold out any sum you've given me from the customary advance."

"When you turn it in.

"I'll turn it in," I said. "Two weeks from today."

He hesitated, swayed against his better judgement. "I don't think you will," he said slowly. "I don't see how you can, even though I'm sure your intentions are good. However ..."

I walked out of that office with a battered typewriter in one hand and a check in the other. I checked out of my hotel, rented a cheap room near Seventh Avenue and Twenty-third Street and went to work. For the following ten days I worked on the average of twenty hours a day, eating next to nothing, sipping occasionally at a bottle of whiskey.

At the end of ten days I had a manuscript of some seventy thousand words, which, with the rewriting I had done, represented an average output of more than fifteen thousand words a day.

I presented the manuscript to the publisher. He read and accepted it on the spot. He also signed a contract with me for two more novels.

Now and On Earth was fictionalized autobiography, leaning heavily on Thompson's aircraft-factory time. War and his own dissolutions ensued, and four years passed before publication of another novel, *Heed the Thunder.* By Thompson's account those years were filled with newspaper jobs, an abortive induction into the armed services, and much drinking. His essay "An Alcoholic Looks at Himself," published in Saga in 1950, begins:

I am writing this with two letters before me.

One, from my literary agent, informs me that the Australian

and French rights to my third novel have just been sold; that, in short, the book is almost certain to make an appreciable sum of money. The other is from a newspaper, firing me from the best job I ever held.

The first letter leaves me strangely apathetic. I worked on that novel over a period of several years; it has little bearing on my present ability to write another; and I owe far more money than any extravagant sum I might receive from it.

I hold the second letter in exactly as much esteem as I do my life.

For more than a decade then, Jim Thompson turned out paperback novels, at least twenty-nine of them, thirteen in one amazing four-year period from 1952 to 1956. Polito and McCauley warn, however, against visions of the novelist hacking steadily away behind closed doors:

Although his legend glows with the heat of his unrelenting industry, actually he tended to supplement protracted quiescent stretches with booming bursts of productivity in which he might dispatch a novel or half-dozen magazine features in less than a month. Mingling sleek, calculated compositions and commissioned pieces tossed off for quick money, Fireworks inevitably also documents Thompson's unsteady negotiations with the literary marketplace and his improvised, often precarious working life. For every bravura effort that demonstrates steady deliberation and revision, there are many more junkyard gems cut hastily under preposterous conditions.

Its social position and purpose largely usurped by television, by the Sixties pulp and paperback fiction was little in demand, and Jim Thompson lost the only audience he'd had. He tried to adapt, signing on for piecework with *Dr. Kildare* and other, long-forgotten TV series; began and abandoned at least fourteen novels; appeared as Judge Grayles (because he needed the money, but also, surely, in homage) in the 1975 remake of Chandler's *Farewell, My Lovely*. Beginning that same year, he suffered a series of strokes that left him unable to write, yet saw three of his books become films: *The Getaway*, *The Killer Inside Me*, and (as *Coup De Torchon*) *Pop. 1280*.

Jim Thompson died on April 7, 1977.

• • •

In *Nothing More Than Murder*, the first Thompson mystery and also the first of his typical novels, an insurance agent tells wife-killer Joe Wilmot a story emblematic of all Thompson's work.

> It was a murder, Joe. Just about the messiest job I've ever seen. A woman was literally clawed, clawed and chewed to death. Obviously, the murderer was a degenerate or a lunatic; we needed an expert on morbid psychology to get to the bottom of the crime. One of the best men in the country lived right there in the neighborhood, so, with the permission of the authorities, we called him in.
>
> Well, the police threw out the well-known dragnet, pulled in all the twist-brains they could lay hands on, and this guy went to work. And, Joe, by God, it was enough to make your flesh crawl to watch him. He'd sit there in a cell with some bird that you and I wouldn't touch with a ten-foot pole—the sort of bird that does things a lot of newspapers won't print—and he'd pal right up to him. He'd talk to him like a long lost brother. He'd find out what special sort of craziness this guy went in for, and for the time being he'd be the same way. If you closed your eyes and listened, you wouldn't know which one was doing the talking. And, yet, he was one of the most likable guys I've ever known. He talked my language, too. We seemed to click.
>
> We got to where we saw quite a bit of each other outside of the line of business. He'd drop in on me a night or two a week, or I'd run in on him.. We'd have a few drinks and a bite to eat, and bat the breeze around. And, gradually, without knowing I was doing it, I began to get his guard down. He started tipping his hand …
>
> He had a big German shepherd, Joe; a big brute that was a hell of a lot more wolf than it was dog. And I began to notice—

he and that dog were a lot alike. Sometimes he'd snap at a sandwich or a piece of food just like the dog. Sometimes there'd be a trace of a growl in his voice, or he'd scratch the back of his head with that stiff, rapid stroke a dog uses. Sometimes they even looked alike.

The payoff came one night when he started to play with the dog. It started off as a romp, but before it was over they were down on the floor together, snapping and slashing and clawing, yeah, and barking. Both of 'em. And when I got the cops in they turned on us—the two dogs. Wolves. I don't need to tell you who the murderer was.

It's all there: the likableness, the inversion of the criminal into law-keeping forces, the double edge of the dialogue between pursuer and pursued, the spiderwebbed, spreading cracks in civilization's veneer, absolute identification with the other.

Also there is another Thompson signature, a nuts-and-bolt background—in this case, that of film distribution and early movie houses, in other novels that of door-to-door sales, newspaper or oilfield work—whose tangibility starkly contrasts the mythic plights of their protagonists. Since much the same backgrounds turn up in Thompson's supposed autobiographies, we assume direct knowledge, in early years, of such enterprise.

One further signature is the precocity and eccentric brilliance of so many of Thompson's monsters. Autodidact Lou Ford browses through volumes of abnormal psychology in French, German or Italian and works out calculus problems for relaxation; the teenaged protagonist of "A Horse in the Baby's Bathtub" translates Catullus in Sanscrit. Like the backgrounds and rural southwestern settings of his books, this element seems directly appropriated from Thompson's own life. In *Bad Boy* he writes of his early years, when at school he would read "the adventures of Bow-wow and Mew-mew," and at home, aloud to him, the twelve-volume American history given him by his father.

In the same fashion, I was drilled in higher accountancy before I had mastered long division; I was coached in political science before I ever saw a civics class; I learned the dimensions of Betelgeuse before I knew my own hat size. I was always a puzzle and a plague to my teachers. I often knew things that they didn't but seldom anything that I should.

• • •

Sometimes, hat pushed back and boots hooked together, he'll loaf around the streets, leaning against a store front, looking amiable and dull, laughing himself sick inside as he watches the people. Imposing, overblown women and withered-up men. Bowlegged wonders walking alongside knock-kneed marvels. And they're funny, sure, but down below that, underneath, they're tragic. Because life has played a hell of a trick on them all. There was a time, maybe just a few minutes, when all their differences and disabilities seemed to fade away, when they looked at one another just the right way at just the right time and everything came together. They had that time, those few minutes, and they never had any other. All the rest is a long forgetting.

Lou Ford never manages even that connection. His longtime aimless affair with schoolteacher Amy Stanton ("We'd just drifted together like straws in a puddle") is interrupted by Lou's sadomasochistic encounter with hustler Joyce Lakeland, an encounter which tears open internal doors nailed shut fifteen years in the past and places all three non-lovers under an absolute sentence of death.

Thompson hammers away pretty hard at some of this, reminding us both of the haste in which his books were written and the hoary conventions from which they surface. Lou's abnormal, murderous impulses are referred to as the sickness—italicized, as R.V. Cassill remarks, for those who read with their finger. His apartness is also, at least figuratively, italicized by the fact of the vasectomy performed by his own father, by the clichés with which he distances himself from those around him, by the secret lair he's made of his home. Still, Lou's real apartness is from himself, and Thompson charts out the attendant contradictions and correspondences—Lou's gratuitous rage against a bum coupled, pages later, with his kindly disposition of Saturday-night drunks and patient quelling of a violent prisoner, the manumissions implicit in his beating of Joyce Lakeland, the heartlessness and submission of his affair with Amy Stanton—with great care and considerable depth. Like leaves in a bell jar, the two Lou Fords repel one another, and as the charge increases, so does the force. Immolation is the only end possible: the jar must be opened to air.

Here again, R.V. Cassill's observations strike home:

> The reader of *The Killer Inside Me* will have some obligation to spit out the indigestible bones and husks that are part of the literary mode in which this novel was born ...
>
> But what I would like to declare is that in Thompson's hands, the mode of the paperback original, husks and all, turns out to be excellently suited to the objectives of the novel of ideas.

Never intending simple cheap thrills with his portrait of a divided soul, Thompson insists upon showing us "the meaning of the sort we search for when we ask for the meaning of a crucifixion or of the massacre of innocents." Thompson may indeed indulge in putting on scary masks—but first he rips off the faces they go on.

• • •

Throughout the work of all three writers here, of David Goodis (one thinks especially of *Cassidy's Girl*), of Chester Himes (particularly *The Primitive*) and of Jim Thompson, alcohol's husky dark voice reverberates.

It reverberates, in fact, through the entire pulp-paperback tradition, and may, as Geoffrey O'Brien has suggested, be central to it. The typical hardboiled detective novel structurally resembles cycles of heavy drinking, with exhilaration and depression alternating rather predictably, the hero (never more himself than when doing nothing) repeatedly recuperating from beatings which may owe as much to the author's remembered hangovers as to plotline.

O'Brien offers, as example, passages from Kenneth Fearing and Raymond Chandler.

> With a couple more drinks, I felt, I'd have the solution ... There was a plate of grouse and a quart of Scotch. While it lasted, I was a man with a future. And by the time it was gone I'd have the answer to this present jam, an answer that would be perfectly simple ... And then after I'd decided that, I had another drink, and realized I'd been kidding myself. All the way along, not only today, but during the last months, and in

fact, all of my life. The minute a person is born, any person, he is in the middle of a jam, and there is no way out of it except through death.

• • •

I pulled off my coat and tie and sat down at the desk and got the office bottle out of the deep drawer and bought myself a drink. It didn't do any good. I had another, with the same result …

I began to feel a little less savage. I pushed things around on the desk. My hands felt thick and hot and awkward. I ran a finger across the corner of the desk and looked at the streak made by the wiping off of the dust. I looked at the dust on my finger and wiped that off. I looked at my watch. I looked at the wall. I looked at nothing.

Nowadays we understand that there exists an alcoholic personality, components of which are largely interchangeable from individual to individual. Originating in discrepancies between appearance and reality, paralyzed by those discrepancies, this personality is static, spinning out unrealized and unrealizable schemes, expending its energies in placing blame for failure with circumstances and with others, futilely attempting to sustain illusions of coherence in its dissolving world. "Between what seems and what be," John Berryman wrote, "is blinds./Them blinds' on fire."

Though one hesitates to carry this too far, even with the writer's implied validation, several parallels between alcoholic traits and Thompson's preoccupations or recurrent themes suggest themselves. Typically people of high promise and rare gifts, his protagonists never redeem them. They spend a great deal of time—witness Dolly Dillon's self-sorrowful litanies in *A Hell of a Woman*, Lou Ford's disdain of others, Nick Corey's sublimated paranoia— rehearsing these failures. Always there is a profound schism between public and private lives, generally someone who comes upon and threatens to expose this schism. Also evident are an inability to see beyond oneself, endless equivocations, skillful manipulation of others, rage and cruelty to those close by— stepstones of the alcoholic's day.

"When I look back," Jim Thompson wrote, "I find that I have lived in an almost constant state of disappointment, simply because I set my hopes and objectives at ludicrously high levels."

And: "In the earlier stages of my alcoholism I was content with inflicting mental anguish on those near to me. But in recent years, I have become violent. Never have I become embroiled, except accidentally, with someone who might strike back. It has always been with someone who loved or liked me."

We also understand something of the subtle, insidious ways in which those close to the alcoholic themselves become unable to discern what is real, become participants in this revision of the world.

Jim Thompson's family declines to talk about his drinking. He was, they insist, a hard worker, a good provider, a family man. In one secluded room like those to which he often must have retreated in his fifty-plus years as a writer, in the hold as it were, behind locked doors, are the ship's papers, the letters, manuscripts, personal papers and unpublished work that someday may bring us closer to the truth of Jim Thompson's passage.

● ● ●

Halfway through *A Hell of a Woman*, without preamble or explanation, a parallel narrative, "Through Thick and Thin: The True Story of a Man's Fight Against High Odds and Low Women," begins, floating up out of the text like a dead body. The incredible tensions which until this point have held Dolly Dillon in place and together, have begun to tear him apart. Here, in cheapest-pulp pastiche (and certainly with a sense of self-satire on Thompson's part), an alternate truth emerges, a fiction skewed from the "facts" of his life. Later on, this narrative returns, creating for the book a second, subterranean voice, a self as divided as Dillon's own, pulling it asunder until, on the final pages, the two voices come together in alternating lines. This may sound pretentious but, deriving from internal pressures of the book, it works wonderfully—not in some literary journal, but in a paperback book published in 1954 and displayed alongside candy bars, Lucky Strikes and patent medicines.

A passage from *The Killer Inside Me* often returns to memory:

> In lots of books I read, the writer seems to go haywire every
> time he reaches a high point. He'll start leaving out punctuation
> and running his words together and babble about stars flashing

and sinking into a deep dreamless sea. And you can't figure out whether the hero's laying his girl or a cornerstone. I guess that kind of crap is supposed to be pretty deep stuff—a lot of book reviewers eat it up, I notice. But the way I see it is, the writer is just too goddam lazy to do his job. And I'm not lazy, whatever else I am. I'll tell you everything.

But I want to get everything in the right order.

I want you to understand how it was.

And we do understand, in book after book, through thickets of hasty writing and bulrushes of pulp convention, Thompson's unmistakable voice berating and consoling us with its sorrows, its diversions and divergent realities. Critics have held that it was only in rising above their hackneyed characters and contrived plots that Hammett, Chandler or Cain achieved note as writers; surely the point's well taken with Thompson and the other writers here. We most value them because again and again they made, of a common, even threadbare garment, something we had not seen before. Their books are dimestore mirrors whose surfaces get ripped open by shark fins.

In a curious way, O'Brien suggests, it is the paperback's very lightness which enables us to bear the heaviness of what occurs within. Like Dolly Dillon's narrative, the paperbacks were a fantasy of the world about them, at once simplifying that world and retrieving its mystery, investing dim city streets, cheap hotels and dives with a kind of rude poetry, making of them a contemporary and specifically American mythology.

One wonders who but Jim Thompson could manage, and especially in that repressive time, in a magazine-rack novel, to write about a man with no penis, or about incest, or sociopaths.

One wonders who else would think to locate hell in Mexico and then describe it in Dantean detail.

Or to write a novel in which the point of view changes with each chapter.

O'Brien again:

Amid all the mechanical duplication of iconography, a few writers recorded their own visions. The work of these few remains readable to the extent that they made their own variations on the public myth, variations not often noticed in a market equally receptive to the well-worn. These writers make up a strange and melancholy collection of individuals—melancholy at least in part because of the sense of dissatisfaction with their own work that so often emerges. That dissatisfaction, shared by Hammett and Chandler, seems to haunt the hardboiled genre, in contrast to the verve and toughness of the foreground. The great American nightmare of Failure is never far off.

In *Farewell, My Lovely*, Thompson played Judge Grayles, a once-powerful man who, grown old and infirm, does not even protest upon finding his wife in another's arms, but simply drops his eyes and backs out of the room. *I'd used up all the laughter in the world*, Jim Thompson wrote. *I want you to understand how it was.*

In the last years Jim Thompson must have carried with him, to whatever rooms or private places in his mind he withdrew, that sense of failure, that silent retreat. He could not know that his books would have a second life; they'd had so brief a first, and seemed quite forgotten. But now, like past moments that have influenced us in ways we can't quite get hold of, those books have reentered an America where shadows from our hands still climb the walls, recalling shapes we encountered long ago in Jim Thompson's terrible mirrors.

David Goodis: Life in Black and White

Strange, strange stories, from and about David Goodis.

In 1950, age 33, following a prolific New York career as pulp writer, following publication of a first novel at age 21 and seven years later his best-known book, *Dark Passage*, on the wake of which (with its serialization in Saturday Evening Post and purchase as a Bogart-Bacall vehicle) he rode to a six-year contract with Warners, David Goodis returned to hometown Philadelphia where he lived with his parents, a virtual recluse, until their deaths not long before his own in 1967.

In California supposedly he rented a sofa in a friend's home for four dollars a month; that was where he lived. He's said to have driven the same battered Chrysler convertible most of his adult life, sewn labels from fashionable clothiers into cheap suits and worn them till threadbare, then dyed the suits blue and gone on wearing them.

Or he'd stuff the red cellophane from cigarette packages up his nose in restaurants and feign nosebleeds; scream in apparent pain as he went through revolving doors; wear a friend's old bathrobe out into public (one thinks of *Pale Fire*'s poor, mad Kinbote) as "a white Russian, an exiled prince of the blood."

Friends on both coasts recall Goodis frequenting ghetto bars and nightclubs, searching out obese black women who would give him the extreme verbal abuse (and perhaps, from the evidence of his work, more substantial abuses) he craved.

The first sentence of his first novel reads: "After a while it gets so bad that you want to stop the whole business."

So, with the retreat to Philadelphia, began what Geoffrey O'Brien in his introduction to Black Lizard's reissues of Goodis' novels refers to as "a voluntary and secretive descent into oblivion."

There in his parents' home, coursing out some mornings in the old Chrysler, junketing by night into Philadelphia's black heartland, Goodis fixed his gaze on the original-paperback novels coming into their own and began, in book after book, most of them for Gold Medal, three for Lion, a reinvention of the self: a ten-year threnody in which his personal history was rudely transformed into novels about losers, outcasts and derelicts, the unchosen, the discarded. There's no evidence that Goodis had higher artistic goals in mind; he seems simply to have adopted a kind of fiction that would at the same time support him and guarantee anonymity.

With the shift to paperback originals, as though mirroring the failure of Goodis' own ambitions, his books turned exclusively to the underside of the American dream. His protagonists became disgraced, alcoholic airline pilots (*Cassidy's Girl*), artists working as appraisers of stolen goods for burglars (*Black Friday*), once-famous crooners or concert performers reduced by fate and their own innate disabilities to street corner bums or barroom piano players (*Street of No Return* and *Down There*, the latter filmed by Truffaut as *Shoot the Piano Player*).

"In this fashion," O'Brien notes, "David Goodis, great literary artist turned streetcorner hackwriter, could tell his own story and ply his trade at the same time," mapping out a zone in American fiction specifically his, forging novels instantly recognizable for their charged style as much as for characteristic obsessions. The more one reads Goodis' books, O'Brien says, the more insistent becomes the hint of something beyond simple preoccupation or reprisal, something like real madness.

"There are not a dozen books here," Mike Wallington remarks of the author's work in an introduction to Zebra Books' anthology of four Goodis novels: "rather, with remarkable imagination and depth, and not a little madness, he has written and rewritten his one book a dozen or so times."

That book tells, from the inside, the story of a man—artist, musician, pilot—fallen from considerable height, a man who has collaborated in his fall and now embraces it, dulling his loss with alcohol, masochistic relationships, and a passivity reflecting utter disengagement with life.

Two things about all this are truly extraordinary.

First, those twelve books are an unparalleled example of self-revelation in the context or guise of genre fiction, a form not generally thought of as flexible enough for, and indeed rarely bent to, such use.

Second, that such quirky, devil-ridden work could ever have sustained a career as paperback novelist is cause for amazement.

"Nothing so downbeat, so wedded to reiterations of personal and social failure," O'Brien writes, "would be likely to find a mass market publisher at present. The absolutely personal voice of David Goodis seems almost to have escaped by accident. It emanated from the heart of an efficient entertainment industry, startlingly, like the wailing of an outcast."

• • •

There are two well-known photographs of David Goodis.

One shows him in profile, sitting in shirtsleeves and figured tie before a large typewriter, arms out straight and fingers poised as he balances on the edge of his words, the very image of the professional writer.

The other, taken in his room in Philadelphia in 1963, shows him from behind, dark against a light-shot window, in the foreground, on the bed behind him, a book rendered huge by perspective.

• • •

Everything connects in Goodis' world; everything circles back, all streets bear one down to the same dead end. One's past, torn away like a rotting limb, returns in a chance encounter, a woman's face at the window, an opening door. A man's entire life comes down to a stain on the street, to the wrong choice he had to make, to a few seductively shadowed places.

In *Street of No Return* (1954) three bums, "two-legged shadows," sit on a street corner wondering where their next drink will come from. One of them, called Whitey ("The curved glass showed him a miniature of himself, a little man lost in the emptiness of a drained bottle"), wanders off only to return 166 pages later, having relived much of his life—his success as a pop singer and damning, obsessive love for a prostitute, beatings by police, torture at the hands of racketeers who wrecked his throat—and, by turning aside a race riot, having become a momentary hero.

> The three of them walked across the street. They sat down on the pavement with their backs against the wall of the flophouse. The pavement was terribly cold and the wet wind from the river came blasting into their faces. But it didn't bother them. They sat there passing the bottle around, and there was nothing that could bother them, nothing at all.

Virtually every Goodis novel is cut to this pattern. The books and the lives they describe are closed circuits. Something nudges the protagonist's life into motion and for a time, set in motion, it remains so; but the weight of the past pulls it down, slows it, stops it. That return to motionlessness, to safety, is a repose for which the protagonist has paid dearly, giving up all else, and it well may be all he values now.

"Getting down this far, to rock bottom," Mike Wallington writes, "has meant blotting out pain, learning to forget. The dreadful gloom—the foreboding that hangs like a pall over every page of Goodis—is a fear of remembrance."

In *Hardboiled America: The Lurid Years of Paperbacks*, O'Brien notes how, conceived to deal with action and the dynamic interplay of character, the hardboiled novel "tends in fact toward a zero state of silence, solitude, and immobility. If we remove the temptresses and gunmen, we are left with a drab room in which a man alone smokes many cigarettes and empties many bottles of Scotch."

This is Goodis' repose, the destination printed on his characters' bus tickets and stamped into their hearts.

It also highlights Goodis' affinity with other great nihilists of the genre, James M. Cain and Horace McCoy, and suggests one reason the French have so adamantly admired and preserved these writers' books.

Cain's novels open on a world in which desire is all there is. His characters' lives flare to blinding existence around the stabs of this desire then fall back, expended, to ground. *Force of circumstances driving the protagonists to the commission of a dreadful act*, as Cain himself once summed up his concerns—then endless retreat.

McCoy's characters lack even that desire, those bright segments. Gloria in *They Shoot Horses, Don't They* is (O'Brien) "a serene vampire in love with nothingness," in some ways not a character at all but "a borderline of the human personality, beyond which it cannot be said that there is a person there."

It's not difficult to see how postwar French readers came across books like these with a certain shock of recognition. The lack of meaning in it all, the way events just happen—that zero at the center—was very much in the air, simmering into existentialism on Left Bank stoves. In American hardboiled writing, French readers found something both of the intense isolation and anxiety of writers like Gide and Malraux and of the stylistic qualities they so admired (and admire still) in Faulkner, Hemingway, Steinbeck and Caldwell.

The French in fact recognized what no American critic at the time perceived: that stripped-down novels like those of McCoy, Cain or Goodis, trembling at the very edge of the real, all but canceling themselves out in their starkness, gave notice of a world in which mankind skimmed across its surface, finding only what substance the individual might make for him- or herself. France's greatest homage to this new fiction, and one of the great modern novels, came in 1942, seven years after publication of *They Shoot Horses*, with Camus' *The Stranger.*

Perry Miller noted this French affinity in *Atlantic Monthly* in 1951, in a landmark article titled "Europe's Faith in American Fiction," remarking European intellectuals' preference for "violent" or romantic American fiction over the realism of an Edith Wharton or Willa Cather. The vision of these romantics, Miller suggested, matched more closely the European reader's own vision of America and represented, if not the literal, then certainly an important poetic truth. These novels offered, as Gide said, "a foretaste of Hell"—a violent, terrible place quite beyond redemption yet imbued with relentless vitality.

• • •

I am going to America, Svidrigailov says in *Crime and Punishment* just before shooting himself on a street corner.

And so David Goodis returns to Philadelphia.

• • •

Perhaps it's only the true outsider, the sleeper waking in some future world, a Tocqueville, artists like Thoreau or Baudelaire forcing themselves into self-exile, who sees clearly.

There's little doubt of Goodis' outsider status, or that of his characters. And if what he saw beyond that Philadelphia window is flattened, attenuated, reduced to puppet-theater size by his apartness, his preoccupations and his madness, it is also sharply, uniquely defined.

French interest in Goodis has continued unabated. Gallimard kept his books in print even when no English-language editions were available, and in 1984 Editions du Seuil published a book-length study, Philippe Garnier's *Goodis: La Vie en Noir et Blanc.*

Like any biography, Garnier's book is an unrealized quest, part reportage, part detective story. Seeking knowledge of the writer whose books he remembered reading, as a child, in the distinctive black and yellow jackets of Gallimard's Serie Noire, shuttling from New York to Hollywood to Philadelphia, Garnier spoke at length with virtually everyone who knew David Goodis and pulled together a wealth of documentation, atmosphere, and oral history; yet, for it all, at book's end Goodis remains a mystery. Garnier's coda comprises an interview with a black woman with whom Goodis sustained a lengthy relationship in the early Fifties. "The David that she knew," Garnier writes, "was carefree, without armor, without family. And, like the rest, she's convinced that this will-o'-the wisp whom she loved and knew was the 'real David Goodis.' Another one."

Among Garnier's is that with Paul Wendkos, a documentary filmmaker who in the mid-1950s collaborated with Goodis on an adaptation of Goodis' novel *The Burglar*; this became Wendkos' first feature film, and the collaborators became friends. Of all who expressed surprise at the interest afforded his books by the French, Garnier writes, Wendkos was the only one to give this interest serious thought.

> I wonder if the French didn't find a certain existential melancholy in David's novels, an attitude stripped of all judgement toward people touched by destiny in a way that overcomes them completely, but who nevertheless do not lose their dignity, or certain ethical values, or their capacity to feel things. All this despite what life has done to them ... It occurs to me to say that it's a notion totally alien to the American public. His characters never lose their humanity, even if they seem always superficially consumed by despair; they always remain capable of being touched by moral principle, despite their profound disillusion. Surely this is what we find, historically and philosophically, in

46

the French experience following the War. But it's a sensibility all but incomprehensible to Americans, who are forever consumed by optimism ...

I wonder if David didn't write these things completely unconsciously; I am nearly certain that he never thought in such terms. He never spoke of it. I have the impression that for him writing was above all mechanics. A choice of formulas. But despite the formulas, it's inevitable that a writer breathe something of his own personality into even the most commercial projects. I don't know that he ever had the ambition to write "seriously." He didn't talk much, never revealed much of himself, despite a very open, jovial exterior ... Still, he was a remarkable human being, very endearing, who wrote like no one else. The fact that French readers have been able to recognize this, to divine in the eccentricities of his books this unique aspect, says a great deal for French culture, I think.

• • •

Intensity is what one remembers of Goodis, what remains when the water of specific situations and vagaries of plot evaporate.

In a sense, of course, that intensity is his birthright as paperback novelist. In keeping with their covers, these books were shamelessly exploitative, going about their business with bullish single-mindedness. Located at ground zero of popular fiction, paperback novels were single-cylinder machines built to deliver swift, powerful punches. Subtlety and complexity couldn't be allowed to cloud the violent and erotic visions at their heart. Their very meanness elevated them.

Generally, Goodis' command of the mechanics of writing is reliable. The craftsmanship he mastered in all those years of turning out fiction for the pulps, in fact, was sometimes all that salvaged his books from a morass of aberrant psychology and obsession. Goodis knew how to get his characters from room to street, how to carry them along like a good tour guide from the Slough of Despond to Heartbreak Ridge and back again. He knew how to load his sentences, how to hit the ground running. And yet, again, there is something beyond that, something more than craftsmanship, good mechanics, momentum. Again and again Goodis pitches his narrative at so keen a tone that it seems to tremble on some nerve-thin border of terror and fascination.

In a book like *Nightfall*, O'Brien notes, Goodis creates an atmosphere in which everything—the pressing heat of a summer night, a metal box of watercolors crashing to the floor, the winding staircase where words of betrayal are overheard, the mountains towards which the protagonist flees—is at the same time symbolic and sharply, profoundly literal.

This, then is the hyperrealism of the edge: of drink, fever, madness. And indeed, there's a directly hallucinatory quality to such Goodis lines as "The empty room looked back at him" or "quiet came in and sat down," to Parry's conversation with the dead Fellsinger in *Dark Passage* or Vanning's dialogue with his mirror in *Nightfall*. Or the ending of *Down There* (psychiatrists would label this dissociation):

> Then he heard the sound. It was warm and sweet and it came from a piano. That's fine piano, he thought. Who's playing that?
> He opened his eyes. He saw his fingers caressing the keyboard.

These are not mere literary gimmicks; they evolve from particular situations and from characters' intense emotional states, serving as amanuensis to fuller expression. At his best Goodis could make a few careful sentences, a key image or figure of speech, the colors of a room, do a prodigious amount of work. Here, for instance, is the turning point four pages into *Dark Passage*, when passive, innocent Parry, railroaded into prison, betrayed by his presumed friend Fellsinger, takes back his life.

> He was sitting on the edge of his cot. He was looking at the bars of the cell door. Like a snake gliding into a pool a thought glided into his mind. He stood up. He walked to the door and put his hands against the steel bars. They weren't very thick but they were strong. He thought of how strong these bars were, how strong was the steel door at the end of corridor D, how ready was the guard's revolver at the end of corridor E, then the two guards at the end of corridor F, and how high the wall was, and how many machine guns were waiting there along the wall. The snake made a turn and started to glide out of the pool. Then it turned again and it began to expand. It was becoming a very big

snake because Parry was thinking of the trucks that brought barrels of cement into that part of the yard.

Sleep was a blackboard and on the blackboard was a chalked plan of the yard. He kept tracing it over and over and when he got it straight he imagined a white X where he was going to be when the truck unloaded the barrels. The X moved when the empty barrels were placed back upon the truck. The X moved slowly and then disappeared into one of the barrels that was already in the truck.

The blackboard was all black. It stayed black until a whistle blew. The motor started. The sound of it pierced the side of the barrel and pierced Parry's brain.

The book's opening paragraphs, moving Parry quickly into prison, into place for the book's real beginning, are themselves marvels of compression:

It was a tough break. Parry was innocent. On top of that he was a decent sort of guy who never bothered people and wanted to lead a quiet life. But there was too much on the other side and on his side of it there was practically nothing. The jury decided he was guilty. The judge handed him a life sentence and he was taken to San Quentin.

The trial had been big and even though it involved unimportant people it was in many respects sensational. Parry was thirty-one and he made thirty-five a week as a clerk in an investment security house in San Francisco. He had been unhappily married for sixteen months, according to the prosecution. And, according to the prosecution, a friend of the Parrys came into the small apartment one winter afternoon and found Mrs. Parry on the floor with her head caved in. According to the prosecution, Mrs. Parry was dying and just before she passed away she said Parry had banged her on the head with a heavy glass ash try. The ash tray was resting near the body. Police found Parry's fingerprints on the ash tray.

That was half the story. The other half meant the finish of Parry. He had to admit a few things.

Among the things he has to admit are that he hasn't been getting along with his wife, has been seeing other women, didn't go to work that day because of a headache, and is 4-F, unfit to serve his country. Even his name signals defeat: he can no longer turn aside or fend off the blows that befall him.

It's not difficult to see from all this why Goodis has been so attractive to filmmakers. The establishing pace of those first paragraphs, the looping tumble of information, that silk-smooth, imminently visual transition from cell to barrel—all this is quite cinematic. The chilling Parry-Fellsinger dialogue, into which the text moves as smoothly and seamlessly as that snake gliding into a pool, is equally visual and experiential.

There was blood all over Fellsinger, blood all over the floor. There were pools of it and ribbons of it. There were blotches of it, big blotches of it near Fellsinger, smaller blotches getting even smaller in progression away from the body. There were flecks of it on the furniture and suggestions of it on a wall … It was dark blood where it clotted in the skull cavities. It was luminous pale blood where it stained the horn of the trumpet that rested beside the body. The horn of the trumpet was slightly dented. The pearl buttons of the trumpet valves were pink from the spray of blood.

Fellsinger was belly down on the floor, but his face was twisted sideways. His eyes were opened wide, the pupils up high with a lot of white underneath. It was as if he was trying to look back. Either he wanted to see how badly he was hurt or he wanted to see who was banging on his skull with the trumpet. His mouth was halfway open and the tip of his tongue flapped over the side of his mouth.

Without sound, Parry said, "Hello, George."

Without sound, Fellsinger said, "Hello, Vince."

"Are you dead, George?"

"Yes, I'm dead."

"Why are you dead, George?"

"I can't tell you, Vince. I wish I could tell you but I can't."

"Who did it, George?"

"I can't tell you, Vince. Look at me. Look what happened to me. Isn't it awful?"

"George, I didn't do it. You know that."

"Of course, Vince. Of course you didn't do it."

"George, you don't really believe I did it."

"I know you didn't do it."

...

"They'll say I killed you."

"Yes, Vince. That's what they'll say."

"But I didn't do it, George."

"I know, Vince. I know you didn't do it. I know who did it but I can't tell you because I'm dead."

"George, can I do anything for you?"

"No. You can't do a thing for me. I'm dead. Your friend George Fellsinger is dead."

• • •

The vita.

Born in 1917, Philadelphia. Followed in 1919 by a younger brother, Jerome, who dies at age three of meningitis, then, in 1923, by Herbert. Attends Cooke Junior High and Simon Gratz High School, puts in a year at the University of Indiana, then attends Temple University, 1937–38, while beginning to turn out freelance journalism and stories for pulps. Works in public relations locally and, with publication of first novel in 1938, (*Retreat from Oblivion*, Dutton), moves to New York.

Published the year before Chandler's *The Big Sleep*, that first novel is a Hemingwaylike tale of romance and infidelity set against a backdrop of wars in China and Spain. Further mainstream literary efforts are rejected. But for *Horror Stories, Western Tales* and *Dime Mystery Magazine* Goodis produces dozens of stories, a flood of them, also writing whole issues of aviation magazines like *Battle Birds* and *Daredevil Aces* for Popular Publications—as much as 10,000 words a day, better than 5 million words in as many years. He is a regular contributor, as well, to such radio serials as *Hap Harrigan of the Airwaves, House of Mystery* and *Superman*.

In 1942 Goodis surfaces in Los Angeles working for several weeks on a treatment of Destination Unknown for Universal. He meets and marries mysterious Elaine, who leaves him the following year after their return to New York. There is no record of divorce.

Through 1945 Goodis continues churning out stories for the pulps and for radio, becoming associate producer, in fact, for Hap Harrigan.

In 1946 he sells *Dark Passage* to Warner Brothers and steps into a six-year contract with that studio, his contract stipulating that half the year will be spent on stories and novels, the remainder on film work. The following year sees the opening of The Unfaithful with a script by Goodis and of *Dark Passage*, both huge successes, along with publication of *Behold This Woman* and *Nightfall*.

Goodis' career as screenwriter—strange in light of his dramatic gifts, his craftsmanship and the peremptorily cinematic qualities of his writing—is curiously stillborn. He works at various for-hire projects, on an adaptation of Chandler's *The Lady in the Lake*, on an original screenplay which later becomes his last hardcover novel, with Jerry Wald on an epic film concerning the entry of civilization into the atomic age, none of these produced.

Then 1950.

To his credit now are four books. The year of retreat brings a final hardcover, the revamped screenplay *Of Missing Persons*; and the year after, the first paperback original for Gold Medal, *Cassidy's Girl*.

• • •

Probably the most popular of Goodis' paperbacks, *Cassidy's Girl* is a study in failures great and small, written (as O'Brien observes) "in a vein of tortured lyricism all his own, whose very excesses seemed uniquely appropriate to the subject matter." Similarly, Wallington notes that no writer before or since has had so thoroughgoing an obsession with "the shadows cast by the victim, the failure, the drop-out, the has-been"—and *Cassidy's Girl* is where it all came together, where Goodis got the recipe right for this heady stew he'd be brewing up the rest of his life.

There is, first, an environment of grinding poverty. Goodis' people dream *up* to shabby furniture and bad diner food, their poverty yet another manifest of how very near the edge—the edge of everything—they are.

There is then, like a jewel dropped into its setting, or perhaps more fittingly like a beer glass put back in the same stained ring, a sensitive and largely inarticulate protagonist oblivious to his self-destructive drive.

And finally, two women as the horns of his dilemma, one of them hard-drinking and hard-talking, earthy, obese, possessive; the other frail, waiflike, a thing composed of pale, ungraspable dreams, an alcoholic.

The fourth member of the party was someone Cassidy had never seen before. A small, fragile, pale woman. She looked to be somewhere in her late twenties. Cassidy saw her plainness, her mildness. Something kind and sweet. Something sanitary. And yet, as he watched her, as he saw the way she raised her glass, he knew instantly she was an alcoholic.

It showed. He could always tell. They gave themselves away in hundreds of little gestures.

...

She sat there with an empty glass in front of her. She was looking at the glass as though it were the pages of a book and she were reading a story.

...

In the middle of the street they fell again and Cassidy managed to grab her before her head hit the cobblestones. Some light from a street lamp drifted onto her face and he saw that she was expressionless. The look in her eyes was the lost dead look far beyond caring, beyond the inclination to care.

He struggled with her, and again they were on their feet. They moved in a path that had no direction, moving off to the side, then back again, circling and retreating and advancing and finally arriving at the other side of the street and leaning heavily against the street lamp.

As they rested there the damp air coming from the river revived them a little and they were able to look at each other with recognition.

"What I need," Cassidy said, "is just one more drink."

The dead look left her eyes. "Let's buy a drink."

"We'll go back to Lundy's," he said, "and we'll have another drink."

But then suddenly she shivered and he felt the tender frail body quivering against him, sensed the frenzy of her attempt to keep from falling once more. He held her upright and said, "I'm with you, Doris. It's all right."

The protagonist here is James Cassidy, ex-gridiron star, ex-war hero, ex-airline pilot and in many ways ex-human being, a man around whom disaster hangs "like a magnetic, almost seductive aura" (O'Brien). Wrongly held accountable for an airline crash that killed 78 passengers and from which he alone of the crew survived, Cassidy has embarked on a long decline. Now he is married, to blowsy, brawling Mildred, and when not with her tearing up the apartment, or at Lundy's drinking, he drives a bus.

> The important thing was, he had the bus. It wasn't as big as a four-engined plane, but it was a rolling machine, and it had wheels. And he was at the controls. That was the thing that mattered. That was what he needed. More than anything. He knew he had lost the ability to control Cassidy, and certainly he would never be able to control Mildred, but there was one thing left in this world that he could and would control. The one thing that was real, that had meaning and stability and purpose. The thing that allowed him to grip a wheel and shift gears and come as close as he would ever come to the dimly remembered days of piloting a liner in the sky. It was only an old, battered, broken-down bus, but it was a damn good bus. It was a wonderful bus. Because it would do what he wanted it to do. Because once again J. Cassidy was in the driver's seat.

He's *not* in the driver's seat, of course, and will never be. The polar tug of those women betokens divisions within himself. And like most alcoholics, he's able to perceive the world only as a reflection of his own thwarted will. There's a moment near the book's end when Cassidy, caught in the clockwork of an incongruous happy ending, approaches this realization.

> Now he was able to understand the utter futility of his attempt to rescue Doris. There was no possibility of rescue. She didn't want to be rescued. His efforts to drag her away from the liquor had been based on a false premise, and his motive, now that he could see it objectively, had been more selfish than noble. His pity for Doris had been the reflection of pity that he felt for himself. His need for Doris had been the need to find something worthwhile and gallant within himself.

Cassidy's Girl proved extremely popular with readers, becoming one of twelve books published in Gold Medal's first six years to have documented sales in advance of a million copies. (Others include Vin

Packer's *Spring Fire,* John D. MacDonald's *The Damned* and Gil Brewer's *13 French Street.*)

Its hollow resolution is something *Cassidy's Girl* shares with several other novels. *Of Tender Sin*'s impotent alcoholic finds redemption by way of psychological revelation and the wisdom of an old black on Skid Row; the pyromaniac of *Fire in the Flesh* quenches his urge first in cheap wine, then by Freudian insight. But the despair never goes away, O'Brien notes; the works are "suffused with a depression that creeps into the very rhythm of the sentences."

There's little question that Goodis, like Cassidy in the passage above, was projecting his own conflicts, offloading his own summary failures onto his characters. In a sense his novels are a long apology; one, *The Blonde on the Street Corner,* set in the Thirties and relating a writer's destruction by an alcoholic older woman and confrontation with his own sexuality, comes close to autobiography, one suspects.

Witness this paragraph from the first page of *Cassidy's Girl*:

> Aside from the pay, it was emotionally important for Cassidy to do this type of work. Keeping his eyes on the road and his mind on the wheel was a protective fence holding him back from internal as well as external catastrophe.

Isn't this Goodis speaking directly, O'Brien asks—not about driving a bus, but about his own writing? And it's not for style or plot but for this that we read Goodis, he continues, but for this sense of impending inner catastrophe, this all but unbearable intensity that comes to the description of a street lamp or the spill of yellow light through barroom windows, even language itself, with something very close to hysteria.

His books "read like the improvisations of someone compelled to keep writing, to keep the words, the pages, coming toward him. He writes knowing that he must fill the page, finish the episode, continue as far as the next episode, the next book. His central image is always that of the wounded man, his strength gone, pulling himself forward, yet sensing at the same time that he won't make it, that it will all have been in vain."

• • •

What to make, finally, of Elaine, this silent, powerful force in David Goodis' life?

Elaine and he were married less than a year, yet several of David's friends believed him deeply, perhaps fatally, scarred by the relationship. To what degree might the devouring women of his books have originated in, developed from, or echoed his memories and experience of Elaine?

Goodis' cousin remembers Elaine as red-haired, attractive and sexy, but not really well-proportioned, definitely not the mannequin type. She had large breasts and "a glorious posterior," he recalls, and always wore very tight clothes.

Goodis often spoke of Elaine to his friend Jane Fried in later years. "I think it was 1942 or '43 that they were married," she told Garnier. "David said that she wasn't at all the kind of woman he'd expected to marry him. He described her as a 'Jewish princess,' very conventional, hard to please, very chic. I don't know that she was, but she did have that style. Anyhow, it was a complete fiasco. She threw him over pretty quickly; I'm sure she found him too odd, not mature or suave enough for her. She left for New York. He'd go there from time to time to attempt reconciliation. She worked in a fashionable clothing shop and was mortified when he showed up like that to badger her, dressed the way he always was....And David would do it purposely, make himself even more shabby and wretched-looking, and he'd plant himself by the shop-window or the door."

Los Angeles friend Marvin Yolin remembers specific behavior later used by Goodis for a scene in *Behold This Woman*.

"Apparently he was completely overcome by her, and had a terrible time of it. She was red-headed and had large breasts which David adored. When they lived in New York she would wake him in the middle of the night and say: 'You want to see them, you want to see my breasts?' And he would say yes. Then she'd send him off to find her an ice cream, in the middle of the night this is, and of course he'd be gone a long time before getting back. He'd come in with the ice cream then and she'd call him names, curse him for waking her up. He told me that she had rendered him physically and mentally deranged, and even though he was finally able to talk to me about it, and with humor, I'm persuaded that all this had marked him for life."

· · ·

Excepting the hybrid *Of Missing Persons* published in 1950 just as Goodis began his career as paperback novelist, the final hardcover—

following *Retreat from Oblivion* in 1938, *Dark Passage* in 1946, and *Nightfall*, published earlier the same year, 1947—was *Behold This Woman*, the first mining of his own erotic obsessions. "He was barely 30," O'Brien writes, "but his career had already peaked," adding that this "masochist's dream" could not have done much for his reputation. The novel's portrait of a devouring, venal woman is unrelenting, wildly overblown, utterly off the rails.

Philippe Garnier addresses the novel's thoroughgoing wantonness in a chapter given largely to discussion of the milieu of original paperbacks.

> It's the novelistic equivalent of soap opera, and certainly nearer the novels of Cain and "fairy tales for adults" than the world we generally associate with Goodis, that of the gutter and the hopelessly lost. Daydreams are the source of such novels, which describe extraordinary situations, and a special luxury, denied the reader. For Goodis, grand lover of catalogs, such a genre, always written by those with faces pressed to shop windows and showcases, held laughable allure. Since luxury was alien to him, he reduced everything to the paraphernalia of luxury, to its trappings.

Goodis' foppish protagonist, numbering among his preferences blue Oxford broadcloth and Montana Saddle cologne, is "a veritable walking catalog." His counterpart Clara is the kind of woman who sucks all day on chocolates, treats herself to opals and gems, and has a color, complete with outfits and bath salts, for each day of the week. And when he writes of the generous charms of this dominatrix, Garnier notes, Goodis' prose becomes as inflated, unworldly and salacious as any Victorian pornographer's.

> One isn't able to help noticing the sardonic and malicious undercurrents of this curious novel. The tone is extravagant, the details frankly ridiculous, the story absurd and silly. And still, this book perhaps finally tells us more about the man Goodis than all his novels in the Serie Noire. The amount of nonsense in this book is amazing: characters never cease colliding in the most fortuitous and forced circumstances … And of course, characters are regularly knocked down, for

Goodis, even in this novel for housewives, didn't surrender his taste for pugilistic fantasy.

One wonders how such a novel could ever be accepted and published.

The answer lies in Goodis' relative celebrity; he had, after all, major movie sales and serialization in Saturday Evening Post behind him. But the book is really a harbinger of the paperback originals, in which he would be left alone to do pretty much as he pleased. Knox Burger, who took over as editor at Gold Medal, remembers Goodis as being always ill at ease—especially when asked for revisions in a manuscript, something which apparently had not happened before. Burger describes Goodis as timid and socially inept, comparing him to other, more favored Gold Medal writers such as John D. MacDonald and Jim Thompson.

> In my opinion Goodis wasn't in the same league. When I knew him, I think he was trying to do more serious work. He had a lot of ambition, but not the skill, the talent, to pull it off. He was never able to build up much suspense or intrigue because his plots were quite feeble.
>
> In the time of my predecessor Dick Carroll, Goodis was writing his "skid row" novels for Gold Medal. I think those were also an effort towards regeneration. But he wasn't creative enough by then. The well was dry.

● ● ●

Goodis returns to Philadelphia, to 6305 North 11th Street, which will mean to us always now that photograph, its darknesses and aversions. There in his parents' home, dramatic and Goodis-like though this would be, Goodis' life does not end. He moves into the bosom, the center, of his family, making arrangements for the future of schizophrenic brother Herbert, caring for his father, then, following his father's death in 1963, becoming anchor and support for his mother. He goes out to restaurants with old friends like Jane Fried, who gave Garnier a wonderful account of Goodis' last years; meets Truffaut in New York for the 1962 premiere of Shoot the Piano Player; travels briefly to Jamaica and Barbados; continues prowling black nightclubs and carrying on affairs, perhaps imaginary ones, perhaps not, speaking of this continually with friends, concealing it from family.

There are further novels: *Street of the Lost* and *Of Tender Sin* (1952); *The Burglar* and *Moon in the Gutter* (1953); *The Blonde on the Street Corner* and *Street of No Return* (1954); *The Wounded and the Slain* (1955, incorporating scenes from his trip to Jamaica); *Down There* (1956); *Fire in the Flesh* (1957); *Night Squad* (1961).

Each morning Goodis retires to his room and works, breaking off for lunch and a nap, then working on late into the afternoon. His mother guards her son's time, telling all who call: "David's working." He himself rarely speaks of that work other than to remark "I really must finish this thing for Fawcett" or "I've had a rough time of it today."

A long apology, those books, catalogues of infirmities shouted out through narrow windows at the world that had so wounded him, that had allowed him to be so wounded. Alone there he works, driven always and only to fill the page, to find the next scene, the next chapter, the next book. He has to wonder at the task and its purpose. But he has to keep moving, he can't stop, can't look up, can't look away from the wounds, not for a moment.

With his father's death it all starts to fall apart, this one sheltered place he had, this safe harbor. And with his mother's death three years later he seems utterly lost. He seldom works now. In 1965, obsessed with the belief that the producers of The Fugitive have stolen the idea from *Dark Passage*, he brings legal action. In 1966, he admits himself to a psychiatric hospital. On January 7, 1967, at 11:30 P.M., at Albert Einstein Medical Center, age 49, David Goodis dies.

A final Goodis novel, *Somebody's Done For*, is published by Avon under its Banner imprint the year of his death. At that time nothing else is in print in the U.S. Not for twenty years, until 1987 when Black Lizard begins its reissues with *Black Friday*, *Shoot the Piano Player* and *Nightfall*, will another Goodis book surface.

Chester Himes: America's Black Heartland

In one early short story Chester Himes wrote of a black man who, because he will not step off the sidewalk to let a white couple pass, has his feet doused with gasoline and set on fire, consequently losing them. At the end of the story another white man becomes enraged when at a movie theater he fails to stand for the playing of the national anthem, even though it is pointed out that he has no feet.

A later story, "Prediction," opens with the black janitor of the city's Catholic cathedral sitting astride the public poor box with a heavy-caliber automatic rifle, waiting at the end of "four hundred years" while six thousand white policemen parade in the streets below. The ensuing massacre is described with characteristic intensity and shocking detail: rank after rank of policemen are mowed down; shards of bone, lariats of gut and pieces of brains spin through the air. A riot tank is dispatched and, unable to find a target, turns its guns on black plaster-of-Paris mannequins in a nearby store window, then on the policemen themselves, killing 29 and wounding another 117. Finally the black janitor's location is discovered. The tank turns to the stone face and stares a moment "as if in deep thought," then levels the cathedral. But the janitor's symbolic action strikes a resounding blow: "In the wake of the bloody massacre the stock market crashed. The dollar fell on the world market. The very structure of capitalism began to crumble."

These two visions, the naturalist-didactic and the apocalyptic, largely define Chester Himes' career and work. The first of the stories, in its limning of the ways in which white society makes demands on the black which that same society has assured he cannot fulfill, shares with the second a parabolic intensity common to Himes; each suggests, as do his later Harlem detective novels, that the forces of law and order only serve to amplify the disorder and chaos of American urban life. For Himes, the roots of our society are so thoroughly corrupt as to forbid anything approaching normal growth. Though he often has been labeled such, he was not a protest writer, for that term carries an implicit sense of meliorism, or redemptive change, a sense rarely manifest in Himes' work. The sense one does receive is that of a vast pall of futility, a huge sea of inaction and impotence relieved by sudden islands of violent, random motion: the crushing weight of centuries. And his interest from the first had been the individual human consequences of so distorted a society. Of his early naturalism he retained always determinism: if his people are monsters, misshapen, grotesque things, it is because the egg in which they were formed forced them to that shape.

In other respects Himes' naturalism underwent a progression unique to American letters. Reminiscent of Richard Wright and proletarian work of the Forties, the early naturalist novels yielded, with their author's expatriation, to the serial exploits of a team of black Harlem detectives, Grave Digger Jones and Coffin Ed Johnson. These proved quite successful in France and other European countries, in fact winning Himes the Grand Prix Policier, but American publication, at least until quite recently, was perfunctory. Brought out indifferently by various publishers, most if not all these books remained out of print for thirty years or more. Critics typically considered the Harlem books potboilers, pandering to excessive violence and grotesque characterizations, and not a few bemoaned the loss of a talented serious writer. Himes was caught in a curious middle ground: habitual readers of detective stories demanded clear plot and resolution, which he did not provide, and more literate readers (at least in America) believed this sort of ephemera undeserving of their attention. The dilemma was not new to Himes. His second and third "serious" novels had been attacked diversely by white racists, black racists, fascists and the Communist Party. Himes' books were never comfortable spots for the ideologue.

Himes did achieve brief celebrity in 1965 with *Pinktoes*, his satire of black-white (mostly sexual) relations, and in 1970 a popular movie was made from one of the Grave Digger/Coffin Ed books, *Cotton Comes to Harlem*. He then seemed to enter yet another phase, with a two-volume autobiography (*The Quality of Hurt* in 1972, *My Life of Absurdity* in 1976) and a retrospective of shorter work (*Black on Black*, 1973). There was no new fiction, and despite the fact that Chester Himes is arguably among America's most powerful and original novelists, despite, too, a gathering critical acclaim, he remained largely unknown at his death in 1984. Certainly his expatriate status and the biform nature of his work contributed to this, but that work deserves and demands wider recognition. Perhaps no other novelist has so succeeded in capturing the heavy beat of blood, the heaving desperate breaths, of the American city and its inhabitants.

• • •

Years ago, writing about Himes for the first time shortly before his death, I ended in fable.

"It's very sad," his agent, Roslyn Targ, had told me in a telephone conversation. "There's no interest in this country despite all my efforts—none. Yet the publishers every day buy, publish and promote books with not a trace of Himes' power or originality." Money, she told me, trickled in from European editions. As we ended our conversation she asked that I send a letter care of her office, so that Chester Himes would know he remained admired and read.

After speaking with Targ I walked to a nearby bookstore, a supermarket really, with bright lines of new covers receding down the aisles like Burma-Shave signs. The weather, as so often in Texas, was uncertain, sunny one moment, then overcast. I had been reading Graham Greene's autobiography, and as I walked, recalling his references to what critics had called "Greeneland," I realized that there was, just as clearly, and for much the same reasons, a Himesland—a coherent world apart, born from its creator's whole spirit: the Harlem of his detective novels.

It is not sad, I thought, but incomprehensible, that these books remained out of print. This is something a writer lives with, of course, often watching his best work disappear beneath the waves; he learns to live with it. Yet it unmans him in ways nothing else ever can—in ways that Chester Himes, author of *If He Hollers Let Him Go* and *The Primitive*, knew all too well. "Very little is needed to destroy a man," Artaud wrote; "he needs only the conviction that his work is useless."

I walked home in rain. Each day Carol went off to work in Parkland's emergency room and brought back communiqués from our own inner city. Some weeks before, a man had injected himself with novocaine and, using a hacksaw, removed his own arm. Once asked to notify a wife that her husband was shot, the police informed Carol that they could not do so; the house was under surveillance by the sheriff's office, with a drug raid planned for that same night. The wife found out anyway and soon arrived, furious because her husband was still alive and she wouldn't get her $20,000 insurance.

"We are suffering," Henry Miller wrote in *The Wisdom of the Heart*, "from a plethora of art. We are art-ridden. Which is to say that instead of a truly personal, truly creative vision of things, we have merely an aesthetic view."

Chester Himes, I thought then, had no aesthetic view. He really was, to use the title of Life's 1970 profile, a "Hard-Bitten Old Pro," a man who always got the work out, who always saw, if not clearly, then sharply. All he wrote bears an unmistakably personal vision, and the Harlem novels are sui generis, a literary form to themselves.

Seventy-four years old at that time, in poor health and living in exile, Chester Himes remained, as he had always been, a man apart.

Again and again, I wrote then, he has held a mirror to this country, hoping the monster would see itself and feel shame, know what it was. But the monster breaks all mirrors that show true, and its madness finally drives the man from it. He stands far away, on a cliff perhaps, looking down as the monster breaks its baubles one by one, stuffs itself, fouls its nest, steeps in its anger and hatred. Until one day the monster has nothing left, nothing, and desperately it turns its eyes to that cliff. But the man is gone.

• • •

I first came to Chester Himes in the wake of his success with *Pinktoes*. I saw the film of *Cotton Comes to Harlem* in a midtown New York theater shortly thereafter. Reading those books; stepping over bag ladies and drunks asleep in my apartment vestibule or various odd corners of the street; watching the parade of hustlers, wounded and great American glitter as the city always just managed to heave itself up for another day out of night, like a whale onto the beach—somehow all this became of a piece, and after leaving New York I read nothing more of Himes for many years. But whenever I returned on visits, or thought of the city, I remembered those novels.

I admired their singular voice, the precise economy of Himes' imagery and description, the outlandish rightness of his characterizations and the velocity he generated in his narratives, their sheer force of imagination. Even more perhaps, I admired his creation in these novels of a world unto itself—not Harlem, certainly, but a response to Harlem. "I got the story out of the American black's secret mind itself," Himes said.

Always together, Grave Digger and Coffin Ed prowl the streets in their beat-up, souped-up Plymouth, looking like "two hog farmers on a weekend in the Big Town," connecting with a broad network of junkies, stool pigeons, whores and pimps and maintaining law and order primarily by bashing heads and making deals, in the interim shooting off their mouths and identical long-barreled, nickel-plated .38 revolvers on .44 frames. Grave Digger, the more articulate of the two, has smoldering reddish-brown eyes, a "lumpy" face and oversize frame, and always wears a black alpaca suit with an old felt hat perched on the back of his head. Coffin Ed's face, disfigured by thrown acid in the first of the novels, has earned him a second nickname, Frankenstein, and he often must be restrained from impulsive violence by Grave Digger. The two live near one another, with their families, on Long Island. They share a considerable courage, a sure knowledge of street ways, studied flamboyance—and an abiding pragmatism. They know that nothing they can do is likely to have much real effect, and maintain what order there is chiefly by improvisation, threat and brutality, generally adding appreciably to the toll of bodies and confusion. Here is their first appearance, from *For Love of Imabelle* (also issued as *A Rage in Harlem*):

> They were having a big ball in the Savoy and people were lined up for a block down Lenox Avenue, waiting to buy tickets. The famous Harlem detective-team of Coffin Ed Johnson and Grave Digger Jones had been assigned to keep order.
>
> Both were tall, loose-jointed, sloppily dressed, ordinary-looking dark-brown colored men. But there was nothing ordinary about their pistols. They carried specially made long-barreled nickel-plated .38-caliber revolvers, and at the moment they had them in their hands.
>
> Grave Digger stood on the right side of the front end of the line, at the entrance to the Savoy. Coffin Ed stood on the left side of the line, at the rear end. Grave Digger had his pistol

aimed south, in a straight line down the sidewalk. On the other side, Coffin Ed had his pistol aimed north, in a straight line. There was space enough between the two imaginary lines for two persons to stand side by side. Whenever anyone moved out of line, Grave Digger would shout, "Straighten up!" and Coffin Ed would echo, "Count off!" If the offender didn't straighten up the line immediately, one of the detectives would shoot into the air. The couples in the queue would close together as though pressed between two concrete walls. Folks in Harlem believed that Grave Digger Jones and Coffin Ed would shoot a man stone dead for not standing straight in a line.

In a later novel, urged by their Lieutenant to "play it safe" and avoid unnecessary violence, Grave Digger responds: "We've got the highest crime rate on earth among the colored people in Harlem. And there ain't but three things to do about it: Make the criminals pay for it—you don't want to do that; pay the people enough to live decently—you ain't going to do that; so all that's left is let 'em eat one another up."

As H. Bruce Franklin points out in an excellent piece on Himes in *The Victim as Criminal and Artist*, the variety of violence inflicted on blacks by blacks, finally represented by the two detectives as much as by the criminals they chase, becomes the persistent theme of the Harlem novels. But, he adds, these two black cops know who the real enemy is. In *The Real Cool Killers*, after a rare exercise of traditional detective methods to discover the killer, Grave Digger conceals her identity, chiefly because she is one of the rare Harlem inhabitants who has struck back—in this case against a wealthy white sadist who comes uptown to beat young girls.

Though the Harlem novels develop in a fairly clear line from the modern detective novel as established by Hammett (particularly *Red Harvest*) and Chandler, they were never true genre pieces, fulfilling few traditional expectations, and as they continued, they in fact withdrew ever further from preconceived notions of the detective story. Specific crimes are solved in the early books (albeit rather incidentally), but there is a progressive movement towards concentration on the scene itself, on Harlem as symbol, using the detective story framework as vehicle for character and social portraiture. As this shift occurs, absurdities, incomprehensible events and grotesqueries proliferate. The books close on greater disorder and confusion than they began with, as James Lundquist observes in his book-length study of Himes: "Order and reason are left farther and farther behind as the crimes Grave Digger and Coffin Ed must solve and the means of solution become ever more outrageous." This is of course nihilism—and a near-perfect reversal of Gide's description of the detective story as a form in which "every character is trying to deceive all the others and in which the truth slowly becomes visible through the haze of deception."

Himes did not plan this evolution; it grew quite spontaneously out of the material he was working with in the Harlem novels, and out of his own experience. In *My Life of Absurdity* he described writing these novels:

> I would sit in my room and become hysterical thinking about the wild, incredible story I was writing. But it was only for the French, I thought, and they would believe anything about Americans, black or white, if it was bad enough. And I thought I was writing realism. It never occurred to me that I was writing absurdity. Realism and absurdity are so similar in the lives of American blacks one can not tell the difference.

These trends culminate—there was a five-year delay between the final two books—in *Blind Man With a Pistol*, the apotheosis of Himes' detective novels. Assigned to find the killer of a cruising white homosexual, Grave Digger and Coffin Ed roar through a landscape of crazy preachers, children eating from troughs, the cant of black revolutionaries, and a gigantic black plaster-of-Paris Jesus hanging from the ceiling with a sign reading *They lynched me*. (Lundquist has called the first chapter of this book "one of the strangest in American literature.") Neither the original nor subsequent murders are solved; the sole connecting link is an enigmatic man (or men, perhaps) wearing a red fez. The two detectives are confounded and frustrated at every turn: politically protected suspects, payoffs and neatly contrived "solutions," diversionary cleanup campaigns and bureau-cracy. Halfway through the novel they are taken off the case, in fact, and assigned to investigate Harlem's swelling black riots. "You mean you want us to lay off before we discover something you don't want discovered?" Grave Digger asks point blank. But he already knows; they all do, and the rest is little more than ritual dance. This is where Himes' work breaks off most surely from its forebears. With Hammett, Chandler or Ross Macdonald, the corruption, however profound, would at last be penetrated; with Himes, it is so pervasive, its signature so universal, that it cannot be.

Towards the novel's end, in a scene paralleling that of their debut in *For Love of Imabelle*, Grave Digger and Coffin Ed are standing on the corner of Lenox and 125th shooting rats as they run from buildings being demolished. Their function, and efficacy, have been so abridged.

Meanwhile a belligerent black man who wants no one to know he is blind, walking streets and riding subways by memory, has become involved in an argument with a gardener (for whites, of course) who thinks the blind man is staring at him. Soon involved as well are a white truck driver and a black clergyman who intervenes to preach against violence. Attacked by the truck driver, the blind man draws a pistol and fires, killing the preacher. He continues to fire as the subway train pulls into the 125th Street station, then staggers up onto the street close behind the gardener and truck driver, where he is shot to death by white police watching Grave Digger's and Coffin Ed's display of marksmanship. Immediately the cry goes out that "Whitey has murdered a soul brother!"

> An hour later Lieutenant Anderson had Grave Digger on the radio-phone. "Can't you men stop that riot?" he demanded.
> "It's out of hand, boss," Grave Digger said.
> "All right, I'll call for reinforcements. What started it?"
> "A blind man with a pistol."
> "What's that?"
> "You heard me, boss."
> "That don't make any sense."
> "Sure don't."

Thus the book ends on a familiar theme: having abrogated their authority, the Lieutenant absurdly expects his detectives still to function. And just as Himes had discovered in his mythical Harlem a correlative for the absurdity of the urban black's life, so he found a final metaphor for the mindless ubiquity of violence against and within those same people.

• • •

Returning to Chester Himes' work after some years, and following that to the man (for his work, I found, passed from autobiographical novels through the Harlem fables I already knew to direct, if weighted autobiography), I discovered an individual quite as unconforming and cryptic as those in the Harlem novels.

Repeatedly, unaccountably, he let himself drift or be pulled, knowing fully the consequences, into impossible situations, as when he accompanied a singularly callow and unattractive girl friend to her home in Germany. There was about him always a baffling passivity, a disengagement, which reminds us that he spent formative adult years (from age nineteen to twenty-six) in prison. And yet, living in France for many years, he refused to learn the language: clearly a willful defiance. He professed astonishment that his actions often led (quite predictably) to disaster; he remarked that "Nothing happened in prison that I had not already encountered in outside life," yet began his autobiography by intimating that prison left scars too deep for probing.

Himes was not a thinker, and his thought rarely penetrated to any significant level beneath the commonplace. When he did attempt discursive thought, outside his personae at any rate, it was, like as not, puerile, and even in the fiction what he shows often subverts what he says. For he was a marvelous observer and prodigious inventor, working by instinct and feeling towards his singular vision; and that vision cannot be reduced to mere ideas. I don't know of any other American writer who has created vivid, memorable scenes in the quantity Himes has, scenes which are hard-edged and durable like a footprint in cement, and with an astonishing economy of dialogue and language.

A passage from the second volume of autobiography, *My Life of Absurdity*, now seems to me emblematic of Himes' work, his description "of a painting I had seen in my youth of black soldiers clad in Union Army uniforms down on their hands and knees viciously biting the dogs the Southern rebels had turned on them, their big white dangerous teeth sinking into the dogs' throats while the dogs yelped futilely." The terrible ambivalence of the black's place in society, Himes' own bitterness and paradoxical rage, elements of graphic violence and opera bouffe, the contradictory, enigmatic and finally irreducible "message," the clarity of scene: the painting is a virtual mirror image of Himes' work.

He was born July 29, 1909, in Jefferson City, Missouri, and grew up chiefly there and in Cleveland, Ohio. His parents were middle-class, his mother a woman of dignity and iron will, his father a college instructor whose own will seems to have been broken over the years, so that he wound up working distractedly at carpentry. Himes attended Ohio State

University for a time but was asked to leave following a fight in a speakeasy. He then worked as a busboy for Cleveland hotels, becoming involved with the hustling life, drinking, gambling. After two suspended sentences for burglary and bad checks, he was finally sentenced in 1929 to 20–25 years' hard labor at the Ohio State Penitentiary for armed robbery, serving seven years, five months of that sentence before parole.

It was in prison that Himes began to write. His first stories were picked up for publication rather promptly by black newspapers and magazines such as *the Atlanta World, the Pittsburgh Courier,* and *Abbott's Monthly.* Then in 1934 a short story titled "Crazy in the Stir," with a prison number as its only byline, appeared in *Esquire.* Two more of Himes' stories were accepted by *Esquire* before his parole in 1936, and another six appeared there in following years. A few were published also in *Coronet.*

The years following parole were difficult ones. Even with the sponsorship of Pulitzer Prize winner Louis Bromfield, Himes was unable to find a publisher for his novel *Black Sheep*; and though for a time he became employed writing a history of Cleveland for the Ohio Writer's Project, with the encroachment of American involvement in World War II all such WPA programs ended. Eventually he joined the river of blacks flowing towards Los Angeles and the wartime defense industry there, his work in the L.A. shipyards providing the setting (and no small part of the rancor) for his first published novel, *If He Hollers Let Him Go,* published in 1945.

> The alarm went off again; I knew then that it had been the alarm that had awakened me. I groped for it blindly, shut it off; I kept my eyes shut tight. But I began feeling scared in spite of hiding from the day. It came along with consciousness. It came into my head first, somewhere back of my closed eyes, moved slowly underneath my skull to the base of my brain, cold and hollow. It seeped down my spine, into my arms, spread through my groin with an almost sexual torture, settled in my stomach like butterfly wings. For a moment I felt torn all loose inside, shriveled, paralyzed, as if after a while I'd have to get up and die.

During the course of the novel, Bob Jones loses his girl, is demoted at the shipyard, suffers endless humiliation and insult, becomes entangled in a brawl and falsely accused of rape—finally having to enlist to avoid imprisonment. The story is told first-person in hardboiled prose. There's little real movement to it; structured around Bob Jones' enigmatic, terrifying dreams, the book simply moves through a train of situations and events reinforcing the sense of Bob and of his destiny we find in that early scene. "I'm still here," he says at the end: hope and a man's life have been thus attenuated.

Himes' next novel, *Lonely Crusade* (1947), concerned fledgling Negro union organizer Lee Gordon, a man whose marriage is dissolving and who takes illusory refuge with a white mistress. The book is uneven, with lengthy discursive passages and a questionable upbeat ending typical of contemporary proletarian novels, when Lee Gordon decides he cannot blame race for everything and finds his identity with struggling working men both black and white. But the book does track relentlessly the emasculating, the unmanning, effects of racism and, written in an omniscient point of view, is, more than any other of Himes' novels, a novel of ideas. Lee Gordon is in many ways an extension of Bob Jones, but where Bob was paralyzed by the ubiquity of his enemy, Lee Gordon, among Himes' finest characterizations, is adamant in finding ground that allows struggle, and in learning how to fight. This hopeful (or existential) posture is one we will not see again.

Upon publication *Lonely Crusade* encountered misunderstanding and condemnation so nearly universal that Himes fell back into bitterness, gradually losing all confidence in himself. "The manuscripts of both *The Third Generation* and *Black Sheep* were making the rounds of the publishing houses at that time," he recalled in *The Quality of Hurt*, "but I had almost lost interest. That summer I had convinced myself I was a failure as a writer, and poverty and loneliness and our enforced separation had convinced me I was a failure as a husband. After fourteen years of love and marriage we had lost each other."

Himes worked various jobs, first as caretaker at resorts, country clubs and estates, then again as a porter and bellhop, over the next several years. In 1948 he gave an impassioned, brilliant address on "The Dilemma of the Negro Writer" at the University of Chicago. For the next five years he was for the most part unable to write, and in 1952, following publication of his novel *Cast the First Stone* (written sixteen years earlier as *Black Sheep*) and widespread attacks on it, Chester Himes fled to Europe.

Cast the First Stone had been written during and just after his prison experience (some of the material was adapted from *Esquire* stories) and was "the outcome of my personal hurts … and did not contain any reference to my racial hurts." The novel as published in fact substituted a white Mississippian for the original black protagonist. It combines a graphic depiction of prison life with a remarkably sensitive story of the love between two men, Jim Monroe and Duke Dido. *The Third Generation* followed in 1954 and, a year later, *The Primitive*. Each of Himes' novels had been brought out by a different publisher.

Directly autobiographical in inception, *The Third Generation* focuses more on dissension within Negro families than on confrontation with white society, in this regard prefiguring the preoccupation of Himes' detective novels with "the infinite forms of violence perpetrated on blacks by blacks" (to borrow H. Bruce Franklin's words). The novel recounts the coming to manhood of Charles Taylor, son of educated, decorous Southern blacks, and the parallel disintegration of his family under the pressure of modern urban life and insidious racism. The parents are patently modeled on Himes' own: the father a dark-skinned trade teacher at Negro schools, gradually descending to manual work because of his wife's inability to accommodate colleagues and neighbors; the mother light skinned and of genteel background, endlessly spurning her husband and showering her whole affection on their son. Sharing the melodramatic plot turns, sometimes diffuse theme and acute psychological portraiture of the preceding novels, *The Third Generation* represents Himes' most direct assault on the Negro middle class, a group the writer always viewed with suspicion. "The American Negro, we must remember, is an American," Himes said in his address at the University of Chicago; "the face may be the face of Africa, but the heart has the beat of Wall Street." One also is forced to remember Grave Digger and Coffin Ed with their comfortable homes and families out on Long Island, coming in to Harlem each day to commit mayhem against fellow, far less advantaged blacks in their enforcement of white men's laws.

Of the characters from *The Third Generation*, Edward Margolies has written in *Native Sons*: "On the surface, rank bigotry seldom intrudes as the direct cause of their sufferings; they appear to be defeated by their own incapacities, weaknesses, blindness, and obsessions. But Himes makes clear that in order to understand them, one must understand the generations that preceded them, black and white: they are doomed not simply by their own psychic drives but by the history that created them and forced them into self-destructive channels. They are as much the victim of a value system they implicitly accept (and which indeed flows in their bloodstreams) as are men like Bigger Thomas who rebel against the social order." With this restatement of Himes' determinism, with the palpable beat of cataclysm and specific focus on black community, we are moving close to the Harlem novels. The book's title derives from Exodus ("for I the Lord thy God am a jealous God, visiting the iniquity of the fathers upon the children unto the third and fourth generation of them that hate me"), but one remembers also that Himes chose to end his autobiography with these words: "that's my life—the third generation out of slavery."

• • •

Just as the Harlem novels culminate in *Blind Man With a Pistol*, the earlier phase of Himes' career climaxes with *The Primitive*, published the same year (1955) he began writing the first of the detective books. In the story of Jesse and Kriss, a failed black novelist and a woman whose own wounds are just as mortal, Himes found a channel for his feelings about his rejection as a writer, and for an investigation of his obsession with white women and all they represented to him. *The Primitive* is easily the most closely structured and artistic of Himes' novels—"the most intricately patterned piece of fiction Himes ever produced," according to Stephen Milliken in his book-length study. In it, too, we find the first exercise of the Rabelaisian humor which becomes central to the Harlem novels.

The narrative here, though, is anything but comic. Jesse and Kriss circle one another like ritual dancers, first simply using one another to satisfy their own needs, then increasingly turning their feelings of failure and defeat upon one another, each in truth seeking his own destruction: the book ends with Jesse calling the police, having just killed Kriss. Himes' presentation is almost theatrical, with a marvelously sustained mood, a new intensity of characterization and physical detail, and fine, impassioned writing. This is a bleak book, one in which the external world and perceptions of it are increasingly bent to the shape of the characters' own doom. In that bleakness, and with similar pervading tone, flashes of detail and inchoate bursts of energy or motion, *The Primitive* (as, for me, does much of Himes' work) recalls Nathanael West.

In one key passage from this novel, Jesse confronts an establishment, apologist editor:

> Pope's face resumed its customary expression of shame and guilt, like that of a man who's murdered his mother and thrown her body in the well, to be forever afterwards haunted by her sweet smiling face.
>
> "I'm afraid I have bad news for you."
>
> Jesse just looked at him, thinking, "Whatever bad news you got for me—as if I didn't know—you're going to have to say it without me helping you. I'm one of those ungracious niggers."
>
> "We've given your book six readings and Mr. Hobson has decided to drop the option."
>
> Jesse had been prepared for this from the moment he'd read Pope's letter and now, before the reaction had set in, he just felt argumentative. "I thought you were going to cut it."
>
> Pope reddened slightly. "That was my opinion. I like the book. I fought for it all the way. I think all it needs is cutting. But Hobson thinks it reads like fictional autobiography. And he doesn't like the title."
>
> "I Was Looking for a Street," Jesse quoted, turning it over in his mind. "I was looking for a street that I could understand," he thought, and for a moment he was lost in memory of the search.
>
> "He said it sounds like a visiting fireman looking for a prostitute's address," Pope said with his apologetic smile.
>
> Jesse laughed. "That ought to make it sell."
>
> Pope again assumed his look of guilt and shame. "The truth is, fiction is doing very poorly. We're having our worst year for fiction."
>
> "Why not publish it as autobiography then?"
>
> "It would be the same. Hobson thinks the public is fed up with protest novels. And I must say, on consideration, I agree with him."
>
> "What's protest about this book?" Jesse argued. "If anything, it's tragedy. But no protest."
>
> "The consensus of the readers was that it's too sordid. It's pretty strong—almost vulgar, some of it."

"Then what about Rabelais? The education of Gargantua? What's more vulgar than that?"

Pope blinked at him in disbelief. "But surely you realize that was satire? Rabelais was satirizing the humanist Renaissance— and certainly some of the best satire ever written ... this—" tapping the manuscript neatly wrapped in brown paper on his desk— "is protest. It's vivid enough, but it's humorless. And there is too much bitterness and not enough just plain animal fun—"

"I wasn't writing about animals...."

"The reader is gripped in a vise of despair and bitterness from start to finish...."

"I thought some of it was funny."

"Funny!" Pope stared at him incredulously.

"That part where the parents wear evening clothes to the older son's funeral," Jesse said, watching Pope's expression and thinking, "What could be more funny than some niggers in evening clothes? I bet you laugh like hell at Amos and Andy on television."

Pope looked as if he had suddenly been confronted by a snake, but was too much of a gentleman to enquire of the snake if it were poisonous.

"All right, maybe you don't think that's funny...."

"That made me cry," Pope accused solemnly.

"I suppose you think I didn't cry when I wrote it," Jesse thought, but aloud he continued, "But how do you make out that it's protest?"

Looking suddenly lost, Pope said, "You killed one son and destroyed the other, killed the father and ruined the mother ..." and Jesse thought, "So you find some streets too that you don't understand," and then, "Yes, that makes it protest, all right. Negroes must always live happily and never die."

Aloud he argued, "What about Hamlet? Shakespeare destroyed everybody and killed everybody in that one."

Pope shrugged. "Shakespeare."

Jesse shrugged. "Jesus Christ. It's a good thing he isn't living now. His friends would never get a book published about him."

Pope laughed. "You're a hell of a good writer, Jesse. Why don't you write a Negro success novel? An inspirational story?

The public is tired of the plight of the poor downtrodden Negro."
"I don't have that much imagination."

Later, in a scene prefiguring Jesse's murder of Kriss, with "a cry of stricken rage, an animal sound, half howl, half scream," he stabs that manuscript. Jesse is not so much a portrait of Himes himself, Milliken suggests, as of "the man he believed he might easily have become had the sequence of misfortunes that overwhelmed him been just a little bit worse, if the screws had been tightened, ever so slightly, just a few notches more."

The Primitive was written in Majorca, where Himes lived in a series of ramshackle villas with a woman he'd met on the crossing, the daughter of a wealthy Philadelphia family, a Hollander's disaffected wife, a would-be novelist.

I wrote slowly, savoring each word, sometimes taking an hour to fashion one sentence to my liking. Sometimes leaning back in my seat and laughing hysterically at the sentence I had fashioned, getting as much satisfaction from the creation of this book as from an exquisite act of love. That was the first time in my life I enjoyed writing; before I had always written from compulsion. But....for once I was almost doing what I wanted to with a story, without being influenced by the imagined reactions of editors, publishers, critics, readers, or anyone. By then I had reduced myself to the fundamental writer, and nothing else mattered.

Distance had brought Himes one liberation and now, in the work, he found another. *The Primitive*, like Himes' other naturalist novels, is a biting, angry book, but there are also scenes of wild comedy: Jesse pursuing an effeminate male Pomeranian ("He takes after his Papa") through the apartment house, belt in hand; or stumbling drunkenly into and falling atop a white statue, thinking they're bound to call it rape. Jesse's self-awareness and irony suggest a new aesthetic remove from his material on Himes' part, and this sense of perspective is underlined by the continual counterpoint of TV, with its news and images of the external world, flooding into Jesse's and Kriss' closed-off world. (Among these images is a chimpanzee who announces historical events—including Jesse's trial and sentence—before they occur.) And that new freedom intimated by Himes, the simple joy in writing, in invention, more than anything else explains the Harlem novels.

• • •

Pinktoes, published in Paris in 1961 by Olympia Press, and in the U.S. in 1965, is something of a sport. Though it introduces the boisterous comedy that became a signature of the Harlem novels and takes up yet again the author's disdain for the black middle class and fascination with interracial sex, there is nothing else like it in Himes' work. The success of *Candy* and other sexual farces somewhat earlier probably accounts both for this book's existence and considerable popularity. Centered around the activities of Harlem "hostess" Mamie Mason, who believes race relations (and her own social pretensions) best served in bed, *Pinktoes* is a scattergun that misses very few targets.

Most of the novel concerns one of Mamie's parties and its aftermath for two men there, black leader Wallace Wright and Art Wills, soon to become (white) editor for a Negro picture magazine. Plot turns and scenes grow ever more grotesque and outrageous. When Mamie, because Art will not feature her in his first issue, tells his wife that he has proposed to a black woman named Brown Sugar, the wife goes home to mother. Word quickly gets around that white liberal husbands are fleeing their wives for brown-skinned girls and there's a panicked run on suntan lotion and ultraviolet lamps. A company that had been producing a skin lightener called "Black Nomore" prospers with its new product "Blackamoor." White women rush to kink their hair, dye their gums blue, redden their eyes.

With *Pinktoes* Himes responds, in part, to a Thirties satirical novel by black journalist and social critic George Schuyler, *Black No More*, the story of a scientist who invents a cream able to turn black people white, and the social havoc this brings on. Largely overlooked by whites, the novel has endured (albeit with extremely mixed feelings and reactions) among black readers.

The attacks in *Pinktoes* are savage ones, true—and unrelenting—yet in the conscious self-parody of his own obsession with interracial sex, and in the unbridled lampoonery of all he held in contempt, Chester Himes seems to have found a kind of deliverance from the pervasive bitterness and gravity of previous work. In this regard, *Pinktoes* may have helped complete what *The Primitive* began.

Two other books of this period, as well, are summings-up of a kind.

A Case of Rape, written 1956–57, was published in Paris in 1963 as *Une Affaire de Viol* and received English-language publication only in 1980 with a small run from Targ Editions; Howard University Press reissued it for the mass market four years later.

The book, of novella length, springboards from the trial and condemnation of four black expatriates for the rape and murder of a troubled white woman in Paris. The book was close to Himes' heart, and many of the details are from his affair with Willa, the woman with whom he lived upon first relocating to Europe.

In his postscript for the Howard University Press edition, Calvin Hernton notes that while Himes takes great care to define racist and sexual elements in the social backgrounds and personalities of his characters, examining almost clinically the all too individual motives which lead to their collision, his ultimate concern is with the inhumanity and insanity of a morally, sexually degenerate world which allows a woman senselessly to lose her life and four men to be wrongly condemned. The men finally are condemned, in fact, not for specific guilt in the case of the trial, but for their general guilt as black men; and the book's final sentence, "We are all guilty," echoing Dostoevski, is Himes' own final condemnation of society.

Along with its structure as tragedy and pervasive apprehension of doom, *A Case of Rape* shares with *The Primitive* a strong sense of the specific quality of defeat reserved in common for women and blacks by society. Kriss is Himes' finest portrait of woman as victim: demeaned, insulted and exploited, "defeated by her sex, by the outraged indignity of childbearing, menstrual periods, long hair and skirts." The true rape here, Hernton remarks, is the white man's rape of Elizabeth Hancock, the white world's sexist victimization of women in general; Elizabeth has been raped all her life by male standards, Christian hypocrisy, Puritan degradation of the female.

Run Man Run (1959, Paris; 1966, U.S.), Himes' only thriller without Grave Digger and Coffin Ed, lies somewhere between the early naturalist novels and the Harlem novels' stark intensity. Jimmy Johnson, a young black man who's witnessed the senseless, savage murder of two fellow night porters, is being methodically stalked by the murderer, a New York policeman named Matt Walker with a psychotic hatred of blacks.

Himes said that he worked very hard to get everything just right in the book, even giving Walker his own alcoholic blackouts and character traits for greater verisimilitude. But as Stephen Milliken points out, what finally menaces Jimmy is not one sick man in a privileged position, rather "the national psychosis of racism fully exposed."

• • •

It seems clear now that the Harlem detective novels are not the anomalies they were first believed to be and rather than breaking the line of Himes' development, significantly extended it. With them, recurrent themes fell into place and perspective, joining the dark vision of the earlier books to the turbulent comedy that surfaced in *Pinktoes*. Released from the twin burdens of autobiography and social significance (at least in any purely programmatic sense), Himes found the ideal vehicle for his particular gifts. The climate of suspicion, fear and violence so much at the heart of the detective story mirrored Himes' own feelings about the black in American society and allowed him a kind of privileged expression. Grave Digger and Coffin Ed, men of ruthless action, supplanted the passivity of earlier protagonists, and Himes fully embraced life's fundamental absurdity. His Harlem is a Harlem of the mind, a total realization of feeling, thought and instinct—America's black heartland. He had moved from finding to making, from the purely representational to a kind of epic poetry.

Yet the books began quite by chance. On a visit to Gallimard to drop off the manuscript for *Pinktoes*, desperate for money, Himes ran into Marcel Duhamel, who had translated *If He Hollers Let Him Go* into French and was then director of Gallimard's La Serie Noire. Duhamel asked Himes to write a detective story for the series and to Himes' protest that he wouldn't know how responded:

> Get an idea. Start with action, somebody does something—a man reaches out a hand and opens a door, light shines in his eyes, a body lies on the floor, he turns, looks up and down the hall....Always action in detail. Make pictures. Like motion pictures. Always the scenes are visible. No stream of consciousness at all. We don't give a damn who's thinking what—only what they're doing. Always doing something. From one scene to

another. Don't worry about it making sense. That's for the end. Give me 220 typed pages.

Gradually, from an old confidence game called "the Blow" Himes had heard of, the book built itself, pure improvisation. After eighty pages he returned to Duhamel for his opinion and more money. He got both. Duhamel loved the book and told him: "Just add another hundred and twenty pages and you've got it....Keep the suspense going. Don't let your people talk too much. Use the dialogue for narration, like Hammett. Have your people see the description. You stay out of it." It was not to Hammett that Himes turned, however, but to Faulkner, reading *Sanctuary* again and again in what became a virtual rite of preparation for the detective novels. The first was published in 1957 as *La Reine des Pommes* with jacket blurbs from Jean Cocteau, Jean Giono and Jean Cau, winning the Grand Prix Policier the following year.

These books are a singular achievement. There is nothing else like them in our literature, and their author rightly deserves the approbation given another American original, Raymond Chandler. But America never had much room for Chester Himes, and these books were almost lost.

Part of the problem with them, as Edward Margolies suggests in *Which Way Did He Go?*, is that, rather than transcending the formula as Hammett and Chandler sometimes did, Himes carried the pulp-detective view of the world to its logical conclusion in absurdity, making of tough-guy fiction "its own moral, metaphysical and social comment."

In a 1969 interview Himes spoke of an ideal novel:

I would like to see produced a novel that just drains a person's subconscious of all his attitudes and reactions to everything. Because, obviously, if one person has a number of thoughts concerning anything, there is a cohesion. There has to be because they belong to one man. Just let it come out as the words generate in the mind, let it come out in the phrasing of the subconscious and let it become a novel in that form ... Since the black American is subject to having millions of thoughts concerning everything, millions of reactions, and his reactions and thoughts will obviously be different from that of the white community, this should create an entirely different structure of the novel.

Essentially, of course, this is not prescriptive but descriptive: a summary of Himes' own practice, and a template for the Harlem novels.

Himes presents to the critic a battery of specific problems. What, for instance, does one make of the bias of the autobiographies with their patent fictionalization of structure and incidents, and with transcription of some of this material directly into his fiction? How does one engage the question of homosexuality, suggested by much (Himes' family relations, *Cast the First Stone*, his spiritual kinship with women, his vitriol against homosexuals in *The Primitive* and other novels)? How conscious (if conscious at all) was Himes' progression in the Harlem books from grotesquerie and slapstick action to the damning commentary of *Blind Man With a Pistol*?

Far more germane are general problems which have held Himes' work in long abeyance. That work, Stephen Milliken reminds us, is social, personal, symbolic and frankly commercial: bleak tragedy, lusty folk humor, sophisticated parody and satire, storytelling for the sheer excitement of story itself.

The central critical problem presented by the great body of fiction published by the American novelist Chester Bomar Himes is easy to state, difficult to resolve. His work has obvious power. It moves the reader enormously, involves him completely. Yet at all points in every part of Himes' work, weaknesses of the most obvious kind are evident. The author seems continually to be opting for the worst of two possible routes, to be choosing, for example, the more striking effect for its impact value alone, or to be choosing the most tired cliché available in full and triumphant knowledge of its falsity and tawdriness. He can in fact be embarrassingly bad, and yet the apparent weaknesses in Himes' work seem somehow to be essential to the strengths.

Perhaps more than anything else, I am writing in this book about failure. I am also writing about the way our lives may be imperfectly ransomed, as readers, but especially as writers, by literature. And about a particularly American genius for quirkiness, cussedness, for getting things done despite ourselves.

As a species, as a nation, as individuals, our strengths often arise directly from our weaknesses. Bleak as they are, broken as they are on history's rack, Chester Himes' books celebrate one man's struggle against terrible odds—against his own life, time and temperament, against the self-limitations of the very forms he chose for expression— to rescue from what Baudelaire called the quotidian frenzy, fragments of enduring truth.

HITCHING RIDES

Grubs & Truffles

Not long after Karyn and I met, as I spoke excitedly to her of a book I was reading for review, she remarked that I wasn't a critic at all, I was an appreciator, an enthusiast. She was right, and for many years I shared that enthusiasm with readers of such as *the Dallas Morning News*, *LA Times*, *Washington Post* and *Boston Globe*. The last even invited me to contribute a column in which I was able for three years to write about French poets, Polish novelists, crime writers, brokers in arealist fiction of every sort—whatever caught my eye. A reviewer's, a reader's, dream job.

Strange as it now seems, in those days newspapers had whole pages given over to reviewing books, some with hefty tip-in sections. They covered the literary waterfront more or less, and they paid (ah, sweet bird and snows of yesteryear!) very well. Those pages, multiple, faded into pages, single, then to half- and quarter-pages.Many surrendered their real estate entirely, and those that held on severely curtailed their coverage. A handful of reviews bounced on the wires from paper to paper, taking over what land remained. My demi-career as reviewer was over.

But I'd begun receiving messages. Someone had seen that piece I wrote in *the Boston Globe* about George R. Stewart's *Earth Abides*, or my *LA Times* review of a Boris Vian translation, or my piece on Marek Hlasko. Would I be interested in, Would it be possible for me to ...

Why yes, I and it would. We here on Grub Street are always looking for work, guvnor.

The reviewer inside me screaming to get out put on fresh clothes, brushed his hair, and got back to work writing introductions to new editions of books, or brief overviews of a writer's work for journals, program booklets, catalogs.

What you have here is the scooped out pith of all the above. For reasons of space, none of my 45 columns for the *Boston Globe* are included, and only one of my 43 columns (thus far) for *The Magazine of Fantasy & Science Fiction*. Also, knowing this selection will be riding a bicycle built for two with *Difficult Lives*, I've tried to browse for keepers chiefly among writings related to crime fiction.

My great hope, of course, is that something here might lead you to search out Hlasko's *Killing the Second Dog*, to find books by Gerald Kersh or Jean-Patrick Manchette, or to read Shirley Jackson in a new light.

Then, having done his job, this cheerleader can put on his street clothes and go home.

James Sallis
Phoenix
January 2016

Derek Raymond
Introduction to the Serpent's Tail
edition of *He Died with His Eyes Open*
Introduction by James Sallis

Five or six times in a life you come across a book that sends electric
shocks skittering and scorching through the whole of you and radically
alters the way in which you perceive the world. There's a great deal of
talk about books changing lives. The mass of people are as likely to
have their lives changed by a doughnut as by a book. But it does occur.

In 1990, as usual, I was reviewing for a number of periodicals; books
arrived daily by the boxful. It became my habit, as I headed out for afternoon
coffee, to select a book at random from the stack and take it along.

One day I happened to pick up the unprepossessing trade paperback
of a thriller by Derek Raymond titled *I Was Dora Suarez*.

And for three or four hours, I was. Not only youthful Dora Suarez,
who lived and died horribly. I was also taken deeply into the mind of
the nameless detective from "the Factory" who, reading Suarez's journal
and following her trail through tangled London streets, sets out first
to solve then to avenge her murder. And from the first page I was
plunged into the mind—terrifyingly into the mind—of the murderer
himself. His thoughts and feelings became as real to me as the chair
upon which I sit now, writing this.

I put down the book stunned. I was sitting outside and, suddenly,
quite ordinary traffic along Camp Bowie Boulevard seemed fraught

with meaning. Streetlamps came on, dim and trembling in early twilight. I realized that this novel on the bistro table beside coffee, saucer and keys had carved its way into me the way relentless pain etches itself indelibly upon the body.

Soon enough then, mapless but undaunted, I was haunting bookstores old and new on the prowl for other Derek Raymond novels.

They were, and remain, strange things when caught, grotesqueries really, unremittingly bleak, brimming with gruesome physical detail, awash with despair. *In between* books—not quite what you'd want to call literary perhaps, but then, not quite crime novels either.

In the novel you now hold, the nameless detective from London Metropolitan Police's Department of Unexplained Deaths ("the most unpopular and shunned branch of the service") barely investigates the crime. His fascination lies with trying to understand the victim, an agenda that in turn, on the author's part, and especially in *I Was Dora Suarez*, carries you full force into the criminal mind. None of the niceties of civilized banter from this detective, brash and strident with fellow officers, superiors, and the populace alike—and nothing of civilized reserve or restraint in these novels. Body and soul, you are scooped from your world, given momentary flight, then dropped on to the hard ground of a world quite different. You stand, and when you do, you enter the minds of criminals and victims; you become prey and predator.

Often, penetration into those minds yields up a marvelously brutal and strangely gentle kind of poetry, as in this passage from well along in *He Died with His Eyes Open*:

> Unhook the delicate, crazy lace of flesh, detach the heart with a single cut, unmask the tissue behind the skin, unhinge the ribs, disclose the spine, take down the long dress of muscle from the bones where it hangs erect. A pause to boil the knives— then take a bold but cunning curve, sweeping into the skull you had trepanned, into the brain, and extract its art if you can.

Or here, as a friend of the detective in youth, a sculptor, speaks of his art:

> "What I'm always trying to capture," he explained, "is the light, the vision inside a man, and the conviction which that

light lends his action, his whole body. Haven't you noticed how the planes of a man's body alter when he's in the grip of a belief? The ex-bank clerk acquires the stature of an athlete as he throws a grenade—or, it might be, I recollect the instant where an artilleryman in an attack, a worker with a rifle, is stopped by a bullet: I try to reconstruct in stone the tragedy of a free man passing from life to death, from will to nothingness. I try to capture the second in which he disintegrates."

Derek Raymond was the pseudonymn adopted by Robert Cook, a well-born Englishman who spent a great portion of his life in France. Turning his back on Eton and all his birth class implied, he worked for years at whatever menial jobs or scams came to him, writing all the while, learning the secret life of London the way a taxi driver must learn its streets. Soon enough he embraced the crime novel, taking as his subject the dispossessed and faceless, society's rejects: alcoholics, abused women, prostitutes, petty criminals swarming like pilot fish in the wake of sharks. His life's work culminated in the four Factory novels now seen as clear landmarks in British fiction: *He Died with His Eyes Open, The Devil's Home on Leave, How the Dead Live, I Was Dora Suarez*.

It seems to me that Derek Raymond occupies much the same position in England as does Jean-Patrick Manchette in France. Manchette salvaged the French crime novel from the bog of police procedurals and colorful tales of Pigalle lowlife into which it had sunk. "The crime novel," Manchette claimed, "is the great moral literature of our time." For Manchette and his followers the crime novel became not mere entertainment, but a means to strip bare and underscore society's failures. Derek Raymond, godfather of the new UK crime novel, who despite his many years in the French language always spoke of the *noir* novel as the *black* novel, was in full accord. The black novel, he said, shows that the world is something quite different and much harder than what we in ignorance and denial go on insisting it is.

"The black novel ... describes men and women whom circumstances have pushed too far, people whom existence has bent and deformed. It deals with the question of turning a small, frightened battle with oneself into a much greater struggle—the universal human struggle against the general contract, whose terms are unfillable, and where defeat is certain."

The black novelist's characters forever step from rented rooms and wretched tenements "into the vile psychic weather outside their front doors where everything and everyone has been been flattened by a pitiless rain that falls from the souls of the people out there."

In another passage from his autobiography *The Hidden Files*, Derek Raymond wrote about his struggle with the raw stuff of his books. He was writing specifically of *I Was Dora Suarez* here but had in mind, I am certain, all the late novels.

"What is remarkable about *I Was Dora Suarez* has nothing to do with literature at all; what is remarkable about it is that in its own way and by its own route it struggles after the same message as Christ." It was, he professed, "my atonement for fifty years' indifference to the miserable state of this world; it was a terrible journey through my own guilt, and through the guilt of others."

What is most remarkable to *me* is the way in which books like Derek Raymond's—strong stuff, graphic, unsettling, even repugnant—can bring us in one hand that "pitiless rain" and in the other a shelter against it. No one claiming interest in literature truly written from the edge of the human experience, no one wondering at the limits of the crime novel and of literature itself, can overlook these extraordinary books. Certainly our highest literature is free to deal with a young woman's decision to marry, with a young academic's coming of age, or with four decades in a car dealer's life. But just as certainly it must deal—as do these books, directly and unflinchingly—with what a guard is said to have remarked at Auschwitz: *Hier ist kein Warum.*

There is no why here.

James Lee Burke
Introduction to Scorpion Press
edition of *Pegasus Descending*
Introduction by James Sallis

I've been sitting here wondering which of several hats I might don to write this introduction.

I could play the critic and go on about how the mystery concerns itself with the past erupting into the present, about archetypes and the many ways in which the crime novel retells stories hardwired within us.

I could easily slip into the role of fellow novelist, talk about what it is to live as a writer, tell you how much I've learned from this man.

Or I could take the stage as for many years a fellow Louisianan, a fellow lover and chronicler of New Orleans.

But instead, I'm going to abjure all masks here and come out barefaced.

I am a flat-out, shameless fan of James Lee Burke. If he were a rock group I'd have all the t-shirts, I'd be prowling the Internet looking to buy taped concerts, and I'd be following him from venue to venue in my banger VW or rusted-out Datsun. Can't get enough. The magic never fades. Hell, I once spent two days of a four-day New York trip holed up in my hotel room reading his new novel.

Back in the dim reaches of the past, before I'd published a novel of my own, I reviewed *A Morning for Flamingos* in *The Washington Post*. "Muscular, headlong stories that honor and at the same time expand conventions of the form," I noted then, adding: "It is quite possible that no one writes better detective novels." I'd spent the previous year or so reading Burke's complete works, beginning with the first Robicheaux novel and, having worked my way through those, seeking out older books: *Two for Texas, Lay Down My Sword and Shield, The Lost Get-Back Boogie.* I was not only reading with intense pleasure, I was also going to school. Out of those Robicheaux novels, with their sure depiction of the Louisiana landscape and the parallel lives of the region's several cultures, came my decision to write about New Orleans, as well as evidence for my growing conviction that the crime novel might be the best lens to focus on what we've made of ourselves and our cities here in post-frontier America. And from the earlier novels and the simple example of Jim Burke came the conviction to write exactly what, and as, I wished.

No one else catches New Orleans as does Burke. Few speak so well to the ever-shifting balance between action and contemplation in our lives, or so well address the relationship of personal and public life: how the self is formed by its environment, how that environment is in turn formed by the many selves, often in dire conflict, that constitute it.

And no one else speaks so lyrically, and at the same time so elegiacally, about an America barely hanging on to what once was. Jim's epilogues, which at first you anticipate to be quiet codas, will tear you apart.

In many ways the American South has always felt itself to be a colonized land, out of which perception come the dark humor, the dissembling, and the sometimes subversive, sometimes prideful attempts to preserve culture that we find common to a colonized people. Southern literature's surest origins are in Poe, the first great Southern writer, several of whose stories, such as "The Fall of the House of Usher," may be seen as covert or coded eulogies to the ethos of the antebellum South, to a way of life (as Jim Burke has written) "being consumed on the edges like an old photograph held to a flame."

It is a marginal land, and Burke's are marginal characters, mugwumps all, one leg planted in this country's occult past, one in personal history, weight shifting restlessly forever between the two. Dave Robicheaux searches for honor in a world where southern gentlemen have devolved to good ol' boys; where friends with names like Clete and Bubba and Batist will stiff you and fight you if you call them on it, then turn and fight at your side against impossible odds; where, at every turn, centers refuse to hold, rules forever change.

"But I don't dwell on the great mysteries any more," Jim Burke writes here. "Alafair will be home for Christmas and Molly and I greet each day as lovers just discovering one another. I live in a place where Confederate soldiers in ragged uniforms hover on the edge of one's vision, beckoning from the mist, calling us back into the past, reminding us that the mythos of winged horses and Grecian warriors was fashioned in our collective souls, that our story is that of ancient gods and peoples and their stories are ours."

And once all the talk about Burke's style is done with, once we've exhausted discussion of his sense of place, his role in American crime fiction, his status as Southern writer, this is what remains, the essential James Lee Burke: his reminder that the real terrors, the real struggles, are always personal and private; that the bad guys have faces and families just like the good ol' boys do; that any foothold is precarious and gives way even as you reach for the next.

The individual life, Burke reminds us, is frail, locked forever to the moment's sensations and uncertainties. Yet behind that life—and this is why the bayou and Louisiana's perduring cultures have such presence and become such important metaphors for Burke—is something stretching back to the far reach of history and of being, something which, through bonds and commitments to others, through re-embracing the natural world and its rhythms, we may yet be a part of.

Patricia Highsmith
Essay for *the Boston Review*
The Selected Stories of Patricia Highsmith
by Patricia Highsmith
W.W. Norton, $27.95
by James Sallis

Reject as we will the romantic portrait, insisting on our status as professionals, self-contained factories, literary hired guns, the fact remains that many writers are by nature outriders, social misanthropes of a sort. Just as a certain personality type seems drawn to surgery, so does another find itself early on telling stories to classmates, jotting ideas and thoughts in notebooks meant to hold classroom notes, surreptitiously dropping those first manuscripts in the postbox. A loner and psychologically apart yet committed to communication, often one struggles with oneself and with reader's expectations as much as with the material to hand. This seems particularly true of writers who simultaneously court and challenge genre conventions, people like Theodore Sturgeon, Chester Himes, Iain Sinclair, Jonathan Carroll, Jack O'Connell. There's a gravity forever working to draw down both work and worker. With each new day, each new novel or essay, each new paragraph and page, one must convince oneself that this is worth doing—that what ones does, matters. Stubborness, contrariness, become coin of the realm.

Few more stubborn, contrary or self-assuming writers than Patricia Highsmith. Making no concessions to market forces—perhaps, like other highly individualist, idiosyncratic writers, she found herself unable to do so—she pursued a career unparalleled among contemporaries, baffling readers and critics, many of whom finally threw up their hands. Here in the States, when known at all she was known as a mystery writer. Her books fell from and returned to print in odd cycles, as though editors, recognizing her importance, could not quite leave her alone yet were so disquieted by the work, so intimately troubled by it, that, having extended a hand, in sudden doubt they drew it back.

In Europe, where she spent much of her productive life, and where, as with Gallimard's La Série Noire, genre writing is more likely to be embraced than scorned, Highsmith became widely recognized as simply a novelist, even though, as with many expatriates, America remained her compelling subject.

American literature, of course, bears a heavy heritage of pulpdom, and for the most part prefers lines between low and high cultures solidly drawn. With *Strangers on a Train* and subsequent meta-mysteries, Highsmith tapped into genre energies, but she inflamed also bare-rubbed spots of the American soul others had agreed to leave alone. Her art records the bursting of blisters that come up when shoes of seem (the salesman measured and assured you they were perfect) don't fit the feet that be. She pushed things to the very borders of expectation, civility, civilization and reason—even of humanity. Nothing human is alien to me, a Latin scribe wrote. Much that's human is alien to Highsmith. And if America's tale has always best been told by outsiders, by the frontiersmen, Tocquevilles and Thoreaus among us, by artists who ritually by sheer force of will turn themselves into outsiders, then Highsmith made herself, or found within herself, the perfect outsider.

Half a century before the term came into general usage, Highsmith's work was deeply transgressive, transgressive not only of received wisdom, proscribed behavior and social attitudes, but also of agreed-upon notions of fiction. She makes little concession to supposed axioms of character development, proper motivation, the necessary shape of a story. Narrative lines may diverge sharply on the third or fourth page, or in the second paragraph. Story's end is likely to find us with recomplication in resolution's place. Characters act, even kill, arbitrarily and without reason, as in *Strangers on a Train*, while others for similar lack of reason fail to do the simple, obvious things (such as going to the police or withdrawing) that would save them.

One wonders if she may not in fact be something of the ultimate realist. Her characters refuse to fulfill our expectations. They dodge and duck, shimmy, signify, dive and resurface, trailing behind them like an insect's egg case all the complications, swellings, self-contradictions, paper cuts, codiciles, boils, blisters, burdens and sudden turns of our lives.

"She is a writer who has created a world of her own—a world claustrophobic and irrational," Graham Greene noted in his introduction to 1970's *The Snail-Watcher*, reprinted here. A world without moral endings, as Greene says, dark, and lit by sudden flares of violent action. "Nothing is certain when we have crossed this frontier."

Nothing indeed. Everything in Patricia Highsmith's world is fluid, runny, out of reach. Touch it and it breaks up, rolls sluggishly away in pieces, like mercury. The malleability of identity itself proves a constant theme. Tom Ripley, who not altogether coincidentally deals in art forgeries, is the primary example, of course. David Kelsey in *This Sweet Sickness* creates quite literally a house of lies, a kind of stillborn cocoon in which he swaddles himself. Her characters step between lives, move from fantasy to dailyness and back without so much as wiping their shoes at the threshold. Just as Whitman brought out edition after edition of *Leaves of Grass* in more or less continuous revision, so does America, this great anthology, continually reinvent itself—and so do American lives.

• • •

Always the shape of the life looms like a beggar in the doorway, or mad cousins shut away in Southern attics, behind the work.

Patricia Highsmith was born January 9, 1921, in Fort Worth, Texas, to Jay Bernard Plangman, of German descent, and Mary Coates, of English-Scots descent. Shortly after her birth, the parents separated and divorced; Patricia was raised by her Texas grandmother until the age of six, at which time she joined her mother and stepfather, both commercial artists, in New York. She did not meet her father until age 12 and apparently felt no connection to him. Following a series of separations, Stanley Highsmith and her mother would eventually divorce, though not until after Patricia had graduated from Barnard College and returned to live with them in their Greenwich Village apartment. She wrote scripts for comic books to support herself, turning to more serious literature evenings and weekends.

A story written while at Barnard, "The Heroine," was published in *Harper's Bazaar* and reprinted in *O. Henry Prize Stories of 1946*. Then in 1948, with the sponsorship of Truman Capote, she attended Yaddo, where she wrote *Strangers on a Train*, published in 1950, after six rejections, by Harper and Brothers. Down the hall from Patricia at Yaddo was Chester Himes. Alfred Hitchcock filmed the novel in 1951. Though later reclothed by Czenzi Ormonde, the original script of *Strangers* was written by Raymond Chandler, who, interestingly enough, in a letter to Hitchcock and in these excerpts from his own working notes remarked the story's implausibility:

It's darn near impossible to write, because consider what you have to put over: A perfectly decent young man (Guy) agrees to murder a man he doesn't know, has never seen, in order to keep a maniac from giving himself away and from tormenting the nice young man …We are flirting with the ludicrous. If it is not written and played exactly right, it will be absurd.

During the Fifties and Sixties, while chiefly based in New York, Highsmith traveled to and lived in Europe, Mexico and the American Southwest. Tacit assertion of independence of thought came with publication, in 1952, of a lesbian novel, *The Price of Salt*. Brought out under the pseudonymn Claire Morgan, Highsmith's second novel was reissued under her own name only in 1991. In 1963 she moved to Europe for good, first settling in England, then France, finally, for the last thirteen years of her life, Switzerland.

Highsmith never had much that was good to say of her parents. Asked in a 1980 interview why she didn't love her mother, Highsmith replied, "First, because she made my childhood a little hell. Second, because she herself never loved anyone, neither my father, my stepfather, nor me." The same interviewer asked her if she, with a reputation as a reclusive, had ever attempted to live with someone. "Indeed, but it was catastrophic … So, the pleasures of family life, no, thanks."

In her work there are few successful couples or families. Far more common is the sort of desperate isolation à deux demonstrated by Vic and Melinda Van Allen in *Deep Water*. Attractions occur only in tandem, it seems, with repulsion. The stronger character fully subsumes the weaker. Couples seldom reproduce (the Van Allens are an exception), and parents are as absent as children. Highsmith's characters exist as islands, afloat and apart. Tom Ripley is never happier than when shut away from humankind in his train compartment. Highsmith was herself a recluse, living for much of her life alone in an isolated house near Locarno on the Swiss-Italian border. Tom and Heloise in the later Ripley novels do have a workable marriage, true. And Highsmith's lesbian novels—the marriage of Therese and Carol in her second novel, *The Price of Salt*, and the extended family of her last, *Small g: A Summer Idyll*—offer visions of successful alternatives. But for the most part there is a horror of relationships and, especially, of family.

"Old Folks at Home" may be the ultimate horror-of-family story. Looking to be good people and hoping in some vague way to fulfill themselves, its upper-middle-class couple adopts, not a child, but an elderly man and wife formerly ensconced in a nursing facility. Gradually they come to realize they've forfeited their lives. In order to work, they're forced to move to a rented office; soon thereafter their house, everything they own, goes up in fire as a result of the old folks' smoking in bed. Through it all, though, sinking like stones, they retain their good will. "We'll make it," they tell themselves again and again.

When in "The Kite," a rare story including a child, one parent says to another, "As long as he hasn't been—you know," meaning not masturbation, as we're set up to anticipate, but a visit to his sister's grave, we learn something of the real family values at work. Illusion, the status quo, the silent agreements, must be maintained at whatever cost. It's not flying too close to the sun that brings Daedalus down, not heat at all, but the bone-chill of pretense.

Of a long-past era when short stories were thought as urgent in their own way as novels, or at very least proper employment for the imaginative writer, Highsmith published seven collections, beginning with *Eleven* (1970) and ending with *Tales of Natural and Unnatural Catastrophes* (1987), all but the last, posthumous volume brought out in the UK by William Heinemann. Five of the collections are represented here: *The Animal-Lover's Book of Beastly Murder* (1975), *Little Tales of Misogyny* (1977), *Slowly, Slowly in the Wind* (1979), *The Black House* (1981) and *Mermaids on the Golf Course* (1985).

Early stories have been likened by Russell Harrison, in what is thus far the only book-length study of Highsmith's work, to those of Carson McCullers. They are indeed of similar impress. Several collections, such as *The Animal-Lovers Book of Beastly Murders* and *Little Tales of Misogyny*, congeal about some central conceit. Interestingly, the stories demonstrate far greater variety in subject matter, theme and voice than the novels. They're filled with surprises, sharply drawn intriguing characters, brilliantly realized scenes. One turns the page eager to see what comes next—between as much as within stories. Quite possibly this fine collection, along with Norton's reissues of her novels, will win Highsmith the recognition she deserves. Certainly it should gain her a new cadre of readers.

Still, these stories haven't a great deal in common, Harrison points out, with the mainstream American short story, and strike many chords familiar from the novels: evocations of states of extreme anxiety, displacement of a privileged class, the malleability of history and of identity itself, eruptions of violence, cataclysmic interpenetrations of one world into another.

That last may be the key theme for Highsmith.

When at the end of one story here, having just been pulled, as by a drain, into the occasion of another's death, a man stands imagining his own, we understand not only the importance of imagination to Highsmith and her characters, we understand also that something has begun within this man, and where it will lead. "He stared down a long while, and imagined his body toppling over and over, striking the water with not much of a splash, sinking....But he hadn't even the courage or the despair as yet for suicide. One day, however, he would, he knew. One day when the planes of cowardice and courage met at the proper angle." Does anything better define our ambitions and failures, our much-vaunted freedom and all our much-cherished choices, than that final phrase?

Again and again characters force or insinuate themselves into another's life, altering it beyond recognition. Like black holes, they draw everything, even the very light of those other lives, into them. Tom Ripley's irruption into Dickie Greenleaf's life and gradual assumption of it in the initial Ripley book is the best-known example. But there are many others, Charles Anthony Bruno's annexation of Guy Haines' life in *Strangers on a Train* among them. In *This Sweet Sickness*, David Kelsey will not let ex-girlfriend Annabelle be. He purchases a house and furnishes it just as he knows she would like, then lies abed while masturbating with the thought that "His house had the virtue of never being lonely. He felt Annabelle's presence in every room."

This basic theme of interpenetration resounds throughout Highsmith, novels and stories alike. And while they may first appear so, such intrusions are no simple co-opting or appropriation. Guy Haines is complicit in Bruno's scheme; Dickie Greenleaf becomes, at least for a time, half the equation that is Tom Ripley. As Francis Wyndham notes in an essay in *Lesbian and Bisexual Fiction Writers*, Highsmith's peculiar brand of horror comes less from the inevitability of disaster, than from the ease with which it might have been avoided. The evil of her agents is answered by the impotence of her patients—this is not the attraction of opposites, but in some subtle way the call of like to like. When they finally clash in the climactic catastrophe, the reader's sense of satisfaction may derive from sources as dark as those which motivate Patricia Highsmith's destroyers and their fascinated victims.

More than one critic deems the theme an essential masking, locating the subtext of all Highsmith's work in homosexual suppression and discovery. Certainly there's that—as there is, also everywhere, Highsmith's most unAmerican emphasis on class. No doubt she's a master of misdirection, pointing one way, happening another. This is, after all, what artists do. Nor must we demand that artists be fully aware of these displacements. Often they're out there working without a map, making the plough down sillion shine, *gee*- and *haw*-ing by intuition, instinct, crochet, quirk.

• • •

With the years, Highsmith became ever more like Tom Ripley shut away from humankind in his train compartment, ever more apart. Wilfullness turned slowly, one suspects, towards misanthropy; independence of thought to a kind of intellectual fascism. A curious double vision overtook her. Everywhere she looked now were victims. She cared greatly for none of them but could not leave the trailing, pale stories of their lives alone. She had written almost exclusively of victims, it seemed, people whose lives had been annexed, inhabited. Had *everyone's* life been taken over?

Nowhere is Highsmith's misanthropy more apparent than in *Little Tales of Misogyny*, a series of savage vignettes and character sketches with titles such as "The Female Novelist," "The Middle-Class Housewife," "The Fully Licensed Whore, or, The Wife," "The Breeder," "The Perfectionist."

One begins: "A young man asked a father for his daughter's hand, and received it in a box—her left hand."

Another: "There are lots of girls like Mildred, homeless yet never without a roof—most of the time the ceiling of a hotel room, sometimes that of bachelor digs, of a yacht's cabin if they're lucky, a tent, or a caravan.

Such girls are bed-objects, the kind of thing one acquires like a hot water bottle, a traveling iron, an electric shoe-shiner, any little luxury of life."

And, from "Oona, the Jolly Cave Woman": "She was a bit hairy, one front tooth missing, but her sex appeal was apparent at a distance of two hundred yards or more, like an odor, which perhaps it was. She was round, round-bellied, round-shouldered, round-hipped, and always smiling, always jolly. That was why men liked her."

The stories of *The Animal-Lovers Book of Beastly Murder* by contrast show great compassion, if not for humanity. "Chorus Girl's Absolutely Final Performance," told from the point of view of an elephant, gives us in nine pages the whole arc of that elephant's captive life. Also extraordinarily touching is "Djemal's Revenge," with a camel as protagonist. This story's a marvel of setting and atmosphere as well as of headlong narrative motion. Other tales feature a cockroach (again, in first-person), a monkey, hamsters, ferrets, goats, cats, a horse and a wonderful truffle-hunting pig named Samson.

Compassion persists, even turns humanward, in *Slowly, Slowly in the Wind*, which appeared in 1979, two years after *Little Tales*, four years after *The Animal-Lovers Book*. Stories such as "The Network" and "Broken Glass" feature aged, lonely people with few ties remaining, sequestered and barricaded in their apartments in cities—in a society—changed beyond recognition. It's as though their lives had been lifted from the shelf, drained of all that's vital, and the shell replaced. All the old certainties are gone, there's minority threat all about, and everywhere, like black smoke from factories, an unfocused fear and dread. Highsmith's novels of the decade, *A Dog's Ransom* (1972) and *Edith's Diary* (1977), essay similar embranchments, particularly the latter, which concerns itself rather directly with media manipulation, active feminism, the civil rights movement and anti-colonialism, as in this passage.

7/Nov./54. In New York people say politics don't interest them. "What can I do about it anyway?" This is the attitude government powers in America want to foster and do. News is brief, filtered and slanted. The Guatemalan "uprising" would have been far more interesting if social conditions there had been described and if United Fruit Company's activities had been exposed—by radio and TV. Discussion clubs should be set up all over America to talk about forces *behind* things. We have been brainwashed for decades (since 1917) to hate Communism. *Readers Digest* has never failed to print one article per issue about the inefficiency of anything socialized, such as medicine.

That Highsmith's shadowy tales bear political intonations should come as no surprise. This is, after all, the woman who dedicated her 1983 novel *People Who Knock on the Door*

> To the courage of the Palestinian people and their leaders in the struggle to regain a part of their homeland. This book has nothing to do with their problem.

and *Ripley Under Water*, eight years later,

> To the dead and the dying among the Intifadah and the Kurds, to those who fight aggression in whatever land, and stand up not only to be counted but to be shot.

Also from *Slowly, Slowly*, and continuing Highsmith's investigation of the ever-deepening chasm between rich and poor touched on in stories like "Broken Glass" and "The Network," is a rare divagation into apocalyptic science fiction, "Please Don't Shoot the Trees." Elsie and family live in great privilege in a protected enclave safely tucked away from "the cesspools" of the cities. All is ease and good thoughts; even the children travel to school by helicopter. But forces far more ancient than mankind's relentless tucking-away and smoothing-out are at work. That obliviousness we call peace of mind, we purchase finally at great price.

> It was right, Elsie felt, right to go like this, conquered by the trees and by nature … Now the wind whistled in her ears, and she was falling at great speed. A land mass, big as a continent, it seemed, big as she could see, was dropping—slowly for land but fast for her—into the dark blue waters.

Over time the stories, as do the novels, grow denser, layered, increasingly inhabited by darker, more obscure motives and by subtler forms of subterfuge and supplantation. Accordingly they become harder to pin down, to define. Generally troubling at various subterranean levels, they become ever more so.

Stories from "The Black House" are a bleak lot. It's here that "Old Folks at Home" appears, with its adoption of an elderly couple bringing ruin to the adoptive couple's life. Others like "The Kite" and "Under a Dark Angel's Eye" are as deeply disturbing. But the standout is "The Terrors of Basket-Weaving," a masterpiece quite possibly on the order of Henry James's "The Beast in the Jungle." Discovering an uncanny, wholly unconscious skill while repairing a basket found on the beach, a modern urban woman begins to feel simultaneously aligned in spirit with the entire history and character of her race and somehow at a remove from her daily life. She's in equal measure frightened and entranced. "I feel—as if a lot of other people were inside me besides myself. And I feel lost because of that," she tells her husband. But her feelings and her confusion are far more complex than she can relate. In some curious way she glimpsed transcendence, and, in finally burning the basket, has refused it. It's much that feeling we have in the moment great music ends, just before the noise of the world rushes back in and overtakes us.

> Three weeks after the burning of the basket, her crazy idea of being a "walking human race" or some such lingered. She would continue to listen to Mozart and Bartok ... and she would continue to pretend that her life counted for something, that she was part of the stream or evolution of the human race, though she felt now that she had spurned that position or small function by burning the basket. For a week, she realized, she had grasped something, and then she had deliberately thrown it away ... And in fact could she even put any more into words? No. So she had to stop thinking about it. Yes.

With its sharp sense of alienation from the ordinary, with its ambiguity of motive and emotion, its questions of identity and dark interiority, "The Terrors of Basket-Weaving" seems an ideal vehicle for many of Highsmith's concerns. Here again there's an interpenetration of lives that appears to offer deliverance to, but finally cleaves one from, the common humanity. The protagonist's tremulous, penumbral state of mind gets captured marvelously in a story as complex, unsettling, and finally as unsortable, as her own emotions.

Curiously, each of the stories from *Mermaids on the Golf Course* in some way deals with families. "A Clock Ticks at Christmas" chronicles the dissolution of a marriage from a couple's differences in attitude towards possessions and inability to cross class barriers. In "Where the Action Is," a freelance photographer still living with his parents happens onto the shot of a lifetime, a young woman fleeing from her supposed rapist—a photograph that makes his career and bends the lies that are his life into a new, ever-hardening shape. "Chris's Last Party" touches on the extended family of young creative people taken under wing by an older mentor. In "The Button" a man filled with bitterness towards his Downs-syndrome son and empty of feelings towards his wife kills a man, throttling him as he has often imagined throttling his son, and finds release therein: "He had killed a man in revenge for Bertie. He had superiority, in a sense, one-upmanship. He must never forget that. He could face the years ahead with that."

These stories are also, in Grace Paley's phrase, about enormous changes at the last moment.

The protagonist of the title story, "Mermaids on the Golf Course," happened to be on the grandstand nearby at a St. Patrick's Day parade and instinctively threw himself in front of the President when snipers opened fire. Now he is recovering, but finds everything in and about his life changed. Nothing is as it was, nothing as it seems, and he cannot get a hold on any of it. Like "Please Don't Shoot the Trees" a rare excursion into the literature of the fantastic, "Not in This Life, Maybe the Next" recounts the appearance in a lonely woman's life of a gnomelike creature no one else can see, an appearance that first begins refilling, then empties, that life. In "The Romantic," following the death of her long cared-for mother, a woman dresses in her best, most fetching clothes and sits in fashionable lounges pretending to wait for rendezvous, creating for herself an external life to match the internal. Actual dates only serve to persuade her that her life of mind and imagination far surpasses that of the real. She need not be (as Rilke put it) distracted by expectation. *I prefer my own dates.*

So did Patricia Highsmith. She might dress up to date Mysteries, head downtown to hang out with *noir*, smile at Literature quaffing Merlot at the next table. But she always preferred the life of her own imagination, her own dates. She always knew that was the only place she could rightfully live and work.

Patricia Highsmith
Review for *the LA Times*
The Complete Ripley Novels
by Patricia Highsmith
W.W. Norton, 2008, 5 volumes boxed, $100.00
*The Talented Mr. Ripley, Ripley Underground, Ripley's Game, The
Boy Who Followed Ripley, Ripley Under Water*
by James Sallis

In March of 1954, in a rented cottage in Lenox, Massachusetts, Patricia Highsmith, who had gained considerable acclaim with her first, *Strangers on a Train*, and much attention for her "novel of a love society forbids," *The Price of Salt*, sat to begin a new novel.

"I am becoming a little odd, personally," she wrote in her notebooks about this time. And not long before: "My personal maladies and malaises are only those of my own generation and of my time, heightened."

It's pure conjecture, of course, what may have been going on in her mind as she wrote the first pages of *The Talented Mr. Ripley*. But one wonders if in part she may have conceived the novel as a dispatch from the front—not simply a counterbalance to that image of America being presented in Life magazine and on TV, but as a strike at something more fundamental, an indictment of America's very identity.

Highsmith had always felt estranged from the society around her, and grew to feel ever more so. In 1963 she would relocate to Europe and spend the remainder of her life there.

Our national literature and image, with our lives in hot pursuit, enthrone individualism. We're a strange people, eager at one and the same time to be left alone and to triumph over the world about us, Thoreau and Clint Eastwood riding double, notions of manifest destiny, freedom and all those other big words that make us so unhappy coursing and clotting in our veins. This is the land where Everyman, by force of character, can become The Man.

Tom Ripley's is the Horatio Alger story told from the underside, individualism spun out to its thinnest, keenest edge, the story of a man who achieves all the good things of life—security, status, wealth—not through hard work and earnest middle-American values, but through murder and deceit.

The genius of these novels lies in the manner in which Highsmith lodges us so firmly in Ripley's head that his perception of the world begins to seem almost right to us. We become so immured in Tom's world that, like him, we are unable to see beyond it. We come very close to admiring him; we root for his escape from whatever pursuit or situation dogs him. In her book *Plotting and Writing Suspense Fiction*, Highsmith remarked how completely she had inhabited Ripley's world: "I often had the feeling Ripley was writing it and I was merely typing." The very flatness of her prose reflects Ripley's lack of center and substance, the image of a man whose self resides only in externals.

Dispatched to Europe to bring back a wayward son (in purposeful parallel to Henry James's *The Ambassadors*), Tom Ripley instead befriends, or attaches himself to, that young man. Living in Dickie's world, he feels for the first time a part of the larger life around him, no longer shut out from it, granted the due he's always felt should be his. Then Dickie tires of him and tries to send him away. In a murder that is at once real and a symbolic destruction of self—and, above all else, imminently *pragmatic*, as are all his solutions—Ripley kills Dickie and assumes his identity.

We first see Ripley's imagination in full bloom as he sits aboard ship writing a letter to the father who has funded this trip. What began as a simple thank-you note proliferates, until the table is covered with sheets of paper relating the story of his and Dickie's idyllic life together in Europe. At novel's end, circumstances force him to resume his old identity: "He hated becoming Thomas Ripley again, hated being nobody."

The Talented Mr. Ripley was written in six months. The other four novels appeared over a period of 36 years. Forever too adamantine to repeat herself or to court commercial success, Highsmith used them not to do dirty dozens on the original, as so often occurs in a series, but to dig ever deeper into the mind and vacant soul of Thomas Ripley. The surface of Ripley's life may seem calm, but underneath roils the same stormy gulf—and the surface itself is a magnificently constructed lie.

In these books Highsmith is like a fine improvisor, playing the melody then going ever farther afield, always reaching, out to the edge and back, looking to see what all is in there.

By the second novel, *Ripley Under Ground*, set six years after the events of the first, Tom Ripley has married into a wealthy French family and occupies a fine home, Belle Ombre, in the French countryside, where one passtime is puttering about in his garden and another is dealing in art forgeries. Threatened with exposure, he turns again to murder. *Ripley's Game* escalates from a slight at a social gathering to a joking recommendation of the slighter as a contract killer, to full-tilt thriller as Tom joins forces with the surprise assassin against Mafia henchmen. *The Boy Who Followed Ripley* holds a mirror to Ripley's own violence and past when a young man with an assumed identity turns up at Belle Ombre to seek Ripley's help, turns out to have killed his father, then is soon kidnapped by Berlin thugs. *Ripley Under Water* came 12 years after the previous Ripley novel and was second to the last of Highsmith's novels. Ripley, once again the unremarkable well-to-do homeowner, is disturbed by phone calls purporting to be from the man he killed in *Ripley Under Ground*, then by a couple who move in next door and, in the course of an evening's dinner, inquire directly about this man. Here the focus is more on the interior, the blandness of Ripley's outward life belied by the memories and terrible anxieties pushing up from below.

Novel after novel, the waters are troubled, masks rearranged on the face, as Highsmith shows us an individual unencumbered by constraints of legality or morality, truly a self-made man, bringing us to silent recognition of the selfsame treacherous longings coiled and waiting in our own hearts.

These are powerful novels for their compelling character and the force of their narrative, certainly, yet still more so for all that goes on beneath. On the surface we have imminently readable, fairly straightforward novels of suspense. But lurking in depths are coded tales of repressed sexuality; ontological questions of identity; an apologue of adolescence mimicking (lying) its way into adulthood; an allegory of the creative imagination and its perils. These are not things that we take away from the reading; rather they are the things that take us, even if unaware, ever more deeply *into* the reading.

Just a few years ago Patricia Highsmith seemed all but lost to the reading public. Then with the refilming of *The Talented Mr. Ripley*, with a fine biography, *Beautiful Shadow*, by Andrew Wilson (Bloomsbury), and with reissues of several novels, the horizon brightened. Norton, which earlier gave us *The Selected Stories* and the first American edition of the final novel *Small g*, with this boxed set makes a high bid for the recognition Highsmith so greatly deserves.

Patricia Highsmith forever pushed things to the very borders of expectation, civility, and reason. If America's tale has always best been told by outsiders, by the frontiersmen, Tocquevilles and Thoreaus among us, by artists who ritually by sheer force of will turn themselves into outsiders, then Highsmith made herself, or found within herself, the perfect outsider. Her characters and her novels refuse to fulfill our expectations; instead, they challenge all that we know. Can there be a higher art?

Paco Taibo
Afterword to *An Easy Thing*
Harpenden: CT Publishing (UK)
"Incomparable Paco"
by James Sallis

Great writers by definition are outriders, raiders, sweeping down from wilderness territories to disturb the peace, overturn the status quo and question everything we know to be true—then gone. Like deranged cousins shut away in the houses of loving families, they are a great bother, an embarrassment, open secrets trembling always at the very edge of violence, out there just beyond the light of these campfires we call civilization.

No one quite knows what to do with Paco Taibo. Even in his homeland of Mexico, he says, he's an invisible writer—by which he means unapproved, subversive, and in which he takes obvious pleasure. Meanwhile a disarming arsenal of books continues to tumble from his pen: literary novels, revisionist history, collections of journalism, fictionalized biographies, political essays, detective stories.

It's for the last that he may be best known to readers on this side of the Rio Grande, for whom his work poses, I think, a particular problem.

The book you're holding, *An Easy Thing*, published in 1990 by the prestigious Viking Press whose editors could hardly have failed to be aware of its radical subtext, introduced Paco's work here. Viking followed up a year later with *The Shadow of the Shadow*, an extraordinary novel celebrating the streetcar workers' strike in 1922 Mexico City. Neither novel earned much of a foothold on publishing's glass mountain, and Paco soon hopscotched over to The Mysterious Press. Most recently, as one by one his books fell out of print—until this first reissue by The Poisoned Pen Press, at least—he's been published, when published at all, by specialty presses such as El Paso's Cinco Puntos, who in 2000 brought out *Just Passing Through*. That novel's fanciful portrait of real-life labor organizer Sebastian San Vicente was an early sketch for *Shadow* and bears every mark of Paco's style: the folding of historical figures into fiction, the persistent, stubborn blurring of boundaries, a tone that trods consistently some unmarked path between the highroad of stridency and the lowlands of melancholy.

It's not only Paco's prolificacy, the variety and very volume of his work, that confuses us. What are we to make of this constant shuttling back and forth from fact to fiction, history to present life, this summa of revolutionary instinct he seems intent upon providing us, Che Guevara rubbing shoulders with Doc Holliday, Mau-Mau with the Musketeers? Is this man a detective-story writer, an avant-garde novelist, the voice of our collective unconscious, a simple contrarian, some half-crazed libertarian Oliver Stone-type, eyes fixed myopically on a handful of moments in history?

U.S. readers in particular, whose knowledge even of their own radical labor movement has been expunged, are unlikely to know much of the general ideas and passions and of the historical movements, specifically Hispanic and Mexican, central to Paco's work. Using the vocabulary available to us, we connect narrative dots, forcing Paco's attitudes and apostrophes to conform, Procrustes-like, to the closest analog we have, the shape of American leftism, unable to perceive it for the radically different thing it is: anarchism. Anarchism, of course, has a long tradition abroad. But we here in the States have never doubted that every other country at its inmost, secret heart wants nothing more than to be just like us. We would make of them all—think that, given the chance, they would make of themselves—little Americas. Further fundamental differences between "American" quiddities and those from which Paco issues, quickly fall into place.

Unlike the realist American novel, perfectly formed loaves of white bread leavened with irony, the Latin American novel has always been quixotic, playful, self-conscious: a heady mix of coarse grains thrown together on the griddle.

What Paco does, it seems to me, is restore the balance between fabulation and objective social realism. Refusing to dispense with the representational, he refuses also to lash its materials to the mast of likelihood and verisimilitude. Grittily realistic depictions of Mexico City come stepping from the doorways of pure invention. If he wants to have Stan Laurel witness Pancho Villa's assassination or show Leon Trotsky, exiled in Mexico, laboring over authorship of thrillers (*Four Hands*); if he wants to gather an army of fictive heroes including Sherlock Holmes and the Hound of the Baskervilles, the Earp brothers and Doc Holliday, the Musketeers, the Mau-Mau and the Light Brigade around a victim of the 1968 student-led Mexican uprising (*Calling All Heroes*); if he wants to dovetail Leonardo da Vinci's invention of the bicycle with the theft of a kidney from a Texas female basketball player and usher onstage as investigator a doppelganger of himself or of Hector Belascoarán Shayne (*Leonardo's Bicycle*); if he wants to kill off Shayne and in the next book (*No Happy Ending, Return to the Same City*) resurrect him … well, then, he does.

Whatever the story requires.

Paco on Shayne's resurrection: "His appearance in these pages is … an act of magic … irrational and disrespectful toward the occupation of writing a mystery series … the story told here belongs to the terrain of absolute fiction, although Mexico is the same and belongs to the terrain of surprising reality."

Story is all, then. And so Paco goes on pulling real rabbits from imaginary hats.

Initially, he says, he turned to crime fiction from a desire to escape the experimentalism then rampant, to find his way back to storytelling. Like many others (Roger Simon or Stephen Greenleaf in the States, the amazing Jean-Patrick Manchette in France, somewhat later Columbia's Santiago Gamboa), Paco realized that the crime novel gives space and opportunity to address contemporary society as does no other venue, to recreate the actual textures and presence of street life and social levels about him, the flux of assumption and disinformation that keeps the social order afloat, the rifts between reality and appearance that both individual and society must negotiate again and again.

One further spur. Someone told Paco it was impossible to write a crime novel set in Mexico because the crime novel was by its very nature an Anglo genre. Given that, what choice did he have but to write one? Or a dozen?

Again and again here, I've struck out such formalities as *Taibo* and *the author* in favor of, simply, *Paco*. In the cloisters and hallways of my soul I see him striding towards me in T-shirt and leather jacket, Marlboro in one hand, Coke in the other. Uncomfortable at the table of privilege where, attending an international literary conference, he was seated, Paco has escaped. Paco's flown, Paco's once again out and about where he belongs, where all writers belong, at the world's small, crowded, unkempt tables.

Reading, he tells us, the four or five of us there (for we contain multitudes), reading is the most subversive activity in life. Open any true book and you begin to see the world through somebody else's eyes. Nothing is more redeeming than that, or more dangerous.

He believes, too, in the right to myths, the necessity of them. Speaking about Che and other heroes, even small heroes like Hector Belascoarán Shayne, helps us reclaim other rights: our right to romanticism, to adventure, to the sense that our lives are not shallow but infinitely deep, connected to history and to "all those who have no rights, those who suffer abuse their whole lives, people on the margins, the disinherited, the lepers, the poor, the least of the least."

There's the rabbit and the hat, then. And here's Paco Taibo, writer, magician, small hero. The most important postman of all: the one who delivers you to yourself.

Jim Thompson
Intro for *The Golden Gizmo*
Mulholland Books
Introduction by James Sallis

You're just riding along, attending the myriad small callings of your life—food, work, laundry. Maybe you're on a bus or the light rail heading for the grocery store or the bank or mortuary. And this guy sits down next to you, starts telling you all about his life. His clothes don't fit, not even close. He does something for a living that's off the beaten path. He's a movie projectionist. Or he buys up scrap gold from unsuspecting housewives. And there's this woman, he has to tell you about this woman. As he talks on, you look out a window scarred with graffiti, initials, a dozen years of hard-won breath.

You've just entered a Jim Thompson novel.

We love our bad boys, our wild men, those who refuse to stay within the lines. Through the long nights they whisper in our ears. We can hear them coming up the stairs, down the hall, towards us. For us. And yet we know we're safe.

Few wilder, stranger or less safe than Jim Thompson. "Nobody else," Barry Gifford says, "ever wrote books like these."

The Golden Gizmo was the eighth Jim Thompson novel from Lion Books, published in 1954, two years after *The Killer Inside Me*, but written years earlier, when Thompson was desperate for money and still finding his way in fiction, still polishing picked-up stones. Five novels had preceded it in 1953, and four others shared the ride in 1954. And while it's not classic Thompson on the order of *The Killer Inside Me, Pop. 1280* or *Savage Night*, many of the hallmarks, many of the markers by which we find our way about Thompsonland, are here: off-kilter occupation, whiplash shifts of plot, murkish identities, characters pitched at a hard right angle to the world, impossible couples, enterprises and lives of promise gone begging.

> It was almost quitting time when Toddy met the man with no chin and the talking dog.

That's where we start the ride. Then before we know it we're hurtling towards the guide rails, tottering at the sharp edge of out of control. We quick-step, quick-think and quick-talk our way door to door. There's a purloined gold watch with no innards. A poisonous, alcoholic wife and mysterious, faithful Dolores. An apparent murder. Toddy on the run. Satire-sprung visits to two psychiatrists counterposed with memories of gentle emotions long passed. A band of South American Nazis aiming to shore up a staggering economy with gold harvested from fillings. Toddy and a comic swapping schticks at a strip club. Mid-century L.A. hammered out flat by the weight of sunlight and a thousand cons.

And then, of course, there's that talking, hymn-singing dog, Lassie's L.A.-style evil cousin, Robert Johnson's hellhound. Like Toddy, like all of Jim Thompson's characters—like Thompson's work itself—surviving in the cracks between what we claim and what is, in the cracks we step over pretending they're not there.

The Killer Inside Me is the book most people know, or think they know, Thompson's tale of Lou Ford, the kindly sheriff who'll help a man down on his luck at the drop of a ten-gallon hat in the morning and that afternoon kill his own beloved Amy.

And then I saw the puddle spreading out under her.

I sat down and tried to read the paper. I tried to keep my eyes on it. But the light wasn't very good, not good enough to read by, and she kept moving around. It looked like she couldn't lie still.

Once I felt something touch my boot, and I looked down and it was her hand. It was moving back and forth across the toe of my boot. It moved up along the ankle and the leg, and somehow I was afraid to move away. And then her fingers were at the top, clutching down inside; and I almost couldn't move. I stood up and tried to jerk away, and the fingers held on.

I dragged her two-three feet before I could break away.

Add to that *Pop. 1280*, which substitutes Lou Ford, the lawman as Devil, with Nick Corey, the lawman as self-ordained Savior—demonstrating how little difference there is—and you have a pretty good idea of Thompsonland. And for our closing hymn, from *Savage Night*:

The darkness and myself. Everything else was gone. And the little that was left of me was going, faster and faster.

Genre conventions are in place to protect you. The murders aren't real, blood won't soak into your floors and remain there forever, the thing out on your porch is really just a neighbor wearing a fright mask. Mystery novels and thrillers create a world parallel to your own yet sealed off from it and, whatever the wrack and wreckage, somehow safe.

Thompson, however, will not leave well enough alone. Everything starts out just fine and how it's supposed to. But along about page two or three, there's this…leakage. Something dark and immensely troubling begins coming up through the floorboards, scuttling behind the walls, breathing heavily just out of sight over in the room's corner.

All writing is a war against cliche, not solely cliches of language as we generally think of cliches, but much larger ones—cliches of character, of plot, of narrative choices. No one is better than Jim Thompson at getting us behind enemy lines.

Have a minute?
Something I need to tell you.

And once we're there, once we're settled in, he sucker punches us. Bottoms drop away. There's nothing to hold onto. The safety's off. We haven't entered the twilight zone, we've fallen through thin ice into our own subconscious, into the pool of archetypes from which derive all our myths, all our religions and fairy tales, all the stories we go on obsessively telling ourselves. As novelist R.V. Cassil suggests, we have come across, in a garishly packaged novel sold off drugstore shelves and destined to be thrown away after use like an empty soda can, a novel of ideas.

We've reached our last stop.
When the doors open, please exit.

If you're lucky.

Chester Himes
Entry for *Waterstone's Guide to Crime Fiction* (UK)
"Paging Mr. Himes"
by James Sallis

When first I began writing about Chester Himes, some twenty years ago, every one of his books was out of print here in the States. When he was known at all, he was known for the series of detective novels that included *Cotton Come to Harlem*, eight books often perceived as cynical potboilers, sellouts, rags and bones from a once promising, "literary" novelist. Meanwhile, works such as *If He Hollers Let Him Go, Cast the First Stone, Run Man Run* and his central masterpiece, *The Primitive*, one of America's scant handful of perfect novels, seemed, if not lost, then terminally misplaced. But these books would not go away. They would not be (in Sartre's phrase) gagged by the silence of others. They would not get out of America's face. Every five or six years they'd stutter back into print. Obviously something in Himes' work went on connecting in a very real, very enduring way with readers— readers who had witnessed civil rights and black power movements of the sixties, perhaps; readers who remembered the Watts riots and Rodney King; readers who wonder just how today's inner-city apartheid, this partitioning of the nation, came about. Finally now, readers and critics are catching up.

Today all of Chester Himes' books are back in print. James Lundquist's and Stephen Milliken's admirable early studies have been joined by Robert Skinner's *Two Guns from Harlem*, Michel Fabre's and Skinner's *Conversations with Chester Himes* and a recent biography from Fabre and Edward Margolies. Himes is also featured in, indeed central to, a major new study of African-American mysteries, *The Blues Detective*. Increasingly readers and critics recognize that it's not with Richard Wright or James Baldwin—both securely within the naturalist, European style, both embraced by the academic canon—that we find our surest route to the black experience and contemporary black writing, but with Chester Himes. The fantastical, poetic structure of *The Primitive*, the expressionist grotesques and hyperboles of the Harlem cycle, at once look back to African story-telling forms and forward to contemporary literary forms. Chester Himes is not only a major American writer; he may be our central American black writer.

Himes was born in Jefferson City, Missouri, 1909, to a light-skinned, elitist mother and dark-skinned, bandy-legged father who taught blacksmithing and other commercial arts at Negro technical colleges. Over the years the rift between his parents grew unbreachable. Giving up on high expectations she'd had for his father, mother Estelle seems to have transferred those expectations, and ultimately her profound disappointment as well, to Chester. But Chester could never fit himself to anyone's expectations: his mother's, the university's, the literary establishment's, even his own. At Ohio State he joined the black fraternity and tooled about town and campus in racoon coat and roadster. Soon, though, he was spending time in Cleveland's game and sporting houses. Soon, too, with the kind of reckless, irrational behavior that became a leitmotif in his life, Himes tries to dovetail his two worlds. Taking a group of students to one of his regular haunts, he professes incredulity that both worlds should turn against him, and that subsequently he should be expelled.

Himes fell to running errands and interference for gamblers and hustlers. He also worked various Cleveland hotels as a bellhop; at one of these he plunged forty feet down an open elevator shaft. Recovery was slow, resumption of old habits following recovery almost immediate. A number of skirmishes with the law led finally to a sentence for armed robbery. Himes entered prison at age nineteen. It was there that he began to write. Stories appeared in black newspapers, then, with only his prison number as byline, in *Esquire* . His first novels, *If He Hollers Let Him Go*, *Lonely Crusade* and to an extent *The Third Generation*, were protest novels somewhat in the manner of Richard Wright and others. From the first, though, there were significant differences that set Himes' work apart.

Thematically, for one thing, he wrote of middle class, educated blacks. No Bigger Thomases here. For another, he was a highly original writer, spinning out scenes we've never read before, taking close notice of the world from perspectives rarely encountered, convincing us with the sheer physicality of his writing. Himes' novels were also tightly structured, *If He Hollers* around a series of reflective, ever-mutable dreams, *Lonely Crusade* around a series of philosophical dialogues. Exam question: Choose one word to describe Himes' work.

Answer: Intensity. A book like *The Primitive* immerses us so fully in the experience of its characters that our reaction to the book becomes an almost physical one. For this intensity and informing structure, as well as for his addressing of our most profound social problems, the writers with whom Himes has most in common, it seems to me, is Nathanael West, whose *Miss Lonelyhearts* is another of America's undervalued, almost perfect novels.

The detective novels for which he's best known came about with Himes' relocation to Paris. *Lonely Crusade* had met with poor reception in the States and newer manuscripts wandered New York streets like the popular folk song's boll weevil, just lookin' for a home, while in France Gallimard had published him to great acclaim. Fleeing America's racism, Himes joined a select group of black expatriates. At Gallimard editor Marcel Duhamel's suggestion, Himes wrote his first mystery, which promptly won 1958's Grand Prix de Litterature Policière. The specific genius of these books is hard to define. They began, inasmuch as Himes understood the form, as fairly standard thrillers. But, again, Himes could never live up to expectations. He could never say what he was supposed to; he was compelled to say something else. He'd always been an intuitive writer, burrowing his way to the heart of the matter by feeling alone, by sheer force of will and hard work, by instinct. It would be the same with his detective novels. Improvising like a jazz musician, never knowing from page to page what would happen, he wrote one, then another. Good tunes, solid beat, something you could build on. Precisely what he did.

We're coming to recognise now that crime novels provide *the* urban fiction. Few suspected this at the time the Harlem cycle came out—

few but Chester Himes. In these books Himes found what artist Odilon Redon called a visual logic for the imagination: figures that could bear the weight of his preoccupations with social and racial problems without toppling beneath that weight, a freedom of form allowing him to recreate his own complex vision of America, of its disenfranchised, its disadvantaged and mortally wounded, unencumbered by intellectual baggage or the demands of naturalism. Chester Himes didn't transcend the genre so much as he personally reinvented it.

There's nothing else like these books. Nothing. Nowadays, finally, people are reading up and down the twenty-five-year line of Chester Himes' work. Backwards from *Blind Man with a Pistol* to *If He Hollers Let Him Go*. Forwards from *Lonely Crusade* to *A Rage in Harlem*. Rediscovering Chester Himes in all his complexity, all his unity, all his strength and peculiar weaknesses, all his intensity. Recent critical and popular fashion leans heavily on crutches of simile. Often it seems we care less what a thing is than what kind of thing it is. Books sell because they're like the author's last, new movies are touted as six parts this, half a dozen parts that. American literary history offers few analogs to Chester Himes. Nathanael West I've already mentioned. James M. Cain, a writer at least as fundamental to our literature as Hemingway and Fitzgerald, might prove another. Then there are writers like Jim Thompson, Horace McCoy, Philip Wylie, Theodore Sturgeon, Samuel R. Delany. All of them stand apart, having created something the world had never seen before. This may be the highest praise possible. I suppose it might just as well be taken to certify the peripheral nature of these writers, to underline their outlaw status, but (invoking simile myself) I think of jazz, where just such innovations, just such extensions of tradition, initially rejected, became central.

Reflecting his family's upheavals, giving voice to his own growing frustration and bitterness, Chester Himes' view of the black American experience was a grim one. In 1966, addressing an audience at the University of Chicago on "The Dilemma of the Negro Writer in the United States," Himes noted: .

> If this plumbing for the truth reveals within the Negro personality homicidal mania, lust for white women, a pathetic sense of inferiority, paradoxical anti-Semitism, arrogance,

Uncle Tomism, hate and fear and self-hate, this then is the effect of oppression on the human personality. These are the daily horrors, the daily realities, the daily experiences of an oppressed minority.

Elsewhere, though, sounding remarkably like one of his models, Faulkner, Himes asserted:

> There is an indomitable quality within the human spirit that can not be destroyed; a face deep within the human personality that is impregnable to all assaults … we would be drooling idiots, dangerous maniacs, raving beasts—if it were not for that quality and force within all humans that cries "I will live."

Chester Himes could never say what others expected him to say. It was not the fashion in his day to refuse to dissemble, to point unflinchingly at the situation of blacks in America, demanding response; not the fashion to tell wild, high tales, to insist that raids on Senegambian villages and the Watts riots, the drums of Congo Square and the higher reaches of African-American literature were points on a line. We should listen to Chester Himes. We should have been listening all along.

Waterstone's Guide to Crime Fiction (Brentford: Waterstone's, 1997), ed. Nick Rennison and Richard Shephard

Chester Himes
Introduction to *A Case of Rape*
Carroll & Graf
Introduction by James Sallis

A Case of Rape was written in 1956, in Paris, where Chester Himes, like so many black artists before him, had relocated. The most recent of his autobiographical novels, *The Primitive*, with its harrowing portrait of a doomed, self-destructive black novelist, had just been published by NAL in the States and was pending at Gallimard. Two years later, for the first of his eight books featuring Harlem detectives Gravedigger Jones and Coffin Ed Johnson, Himes would receive the Grand Prix de Litterature Policiere. At the time he was wrestling down a no-holds-barred comic novel called *Mamie Mason*; as *Pinktoes* it would become his only truly successful book.

In his autobiography Himes recalled finding it so difficult to keep *Mamie Mason* funny that he began writing a synopsis for an epic novel about American blacks in the Latin Quarter. It would recount the trial of four American black men for the rape and murder of Elizabeth Hancock, and the efforts of another black expatriate, novelist Roger Garrison, to exculpate them.

Not comedy at all.

In a letter to Carl Van Vechten the following year Himes wrote of "a 72-page synopsis of a book in which I had great hopes" and went on to

125

relate the plot and, typically, the many conspiracies that kept the book from being written.

Make no mistake of it: there *were* conspiracies to silence Himes, though none so concrete and thoroughgoing as he imagined. More that (in Sartre's phrase) he was gagged by the silence of others. Even for his time, perhaps especially for his time, Chester Himes was a dangerous man.

It's called dissembling: the first true art form blacks created in the New World. Because he couldn't say what he meant, the slave said something else.

And Chester Himes always refused to say something else. Born to a dark-skinned, practical father and a light-skinned, socially pretentious mother, he spent much of his early life reprising within himself the conflicts tearing at his home and the black society about him. Imprisoned for armed robbery at age nineteen, he began to write, publishing early stories in black newspapers, then in *Esquire.* In 1945 his first novel, *If He Hollers Let Him Go*, came out to the sad old accompaniment of critical praise, meager sales. Two years later *Lonely Crusade* was published and soundly attacked. *Cast the First Stone*, a prison novel, appeared in 1952, *The Third Generation* in 1954. In 1953 Himes fled the United States. He would reside in Europe for the rest of his life.

There erupted then, out of his rage and self-hatred, out of his pain and confusion, *The Primitive*, a brilliant novel as filled with vitriol, hatred, and spleen as anything ever written. It is his first masterpiece, one of the great American originals. It was also a turning point for him. He had come to Europe as a "serious" novelist; he would remain there as a writer of detective stories.

This is from *The Primitive*. Jesse Robinson, who reels through the novel like a man careening from demon to demon, has just had his new novel rejected. The editor tells him: "You're a hell of a good writer, Jesse. Why don't you write a Negro success novel? An inspirational story? The public is tired of the plight of the poor downtrodden Negro." Jesse answers: "I don't have that much imagination."

Verisimilitude, anyone?

This, too, is from *The Primitive*:

> "My name is Robinson, Jesse."
> "Yeah ... Robinson." Whoever he was sounded as if his pants were filled with lead.

"I'm a nigger."

There was a slight pause before the voice said, "What's that?"

"'Where you been all your life, boy, you don't know what a nigger is?"

"All right! Cut the comedy! What's the beef?"

"I'm a nigger and I've just killed a white woman," Jesse said, giving the address, and hung up. "That'll get the lead out of his seat," he thought half-amused.

Only after many rejections was *The Primitive* accepted for paperback publication by NAL. Other novels circulated among New York publishers with little, mostly no, interest. Himes despaired again of ever making a living from his writing.

Meanwhile, stacking bizarre characters, scenes, and jokes like a house of cards, he labored away at *Mamie Mason* and wrote the synopsis eventually published in French as *Une Affaire de viol* and in English as *A Case of Rape*.

In *Mamie Mason* he was swapping eights and doing dirty dozens off George Schuyler's *Black No More*, a thirties satirical novel about a scientist who invents a cream able to turn black people white. In *A Case of Rape*—as in all his finest work—he was doing somersaults off his own heart.

Published by a small press in 1963, the book, despite Himes's claims that it caused tremendous uproar, went largely unnoticed. Excepting a limited edition of three hundred fifty copies, there was no American edition until that of Howard University Press in 1984.

This was the usual fate of Chester Himes's books in the States. His early novels staggered out bewildered from different publishers, the later ones appeared all but invisibly as paperback originals. When sixteen years ago I began writing about Himes, trying to communicate my enthusiasm for this extraordinary work, not one of his books remained in print here. He seemed wholly forgotten.

People had been trying for a long time to forget Chester Himes. By all accounts (including his own) he was a difficult man: irascible, often mean-spirited, self-contradictory. And from the first he insisted upon saying things that white readers did not want to hear. He said them again and again.

In 1948, asked to deliver a paper at the University of Chicago, Himes carried his wounds onstage and, speaking on "The Dilemma of the Negro

Writer in the United States," shocked and astonished his racially mixed audience. Given the nature of white racism, he said, all American blacks must of necessity hate white people. And if the artist's plumbing for truth reveals within the Negro personality homicidal mania, lust for white women, a pathetic sense of inferiority, hatred and fear and most of all self-loathing, then that is the effect of oppression on human beings. These are the daily horrors, the daily realities, the daily experience of blacks in America.

When he concluded, his stunned audience sat transfixed. There was no applause, no reaction at all. Slowly, one by one, they stood and left the room, avoiding one another's eyes.

I submit to you that this has always been the fate of what Chester Himes had to say.

Little wonder that, on a visit to Paris, Malcolm X made a point of climbing seven flights to Himes's apartment to say hello. Thinly disguised as "Michael X," Malcolm in fact appeared in Himes's final, devastating masterpiece, *Blind Man with a Pistol*.

Looking back as it does to the protest novels and forward to the synthesis he achieved in the Harlem novels, *A Case of Rape* is curiously central to Himes's career and concerns. It was in those last novels, especially in *Blind Man with a Pistol*, that he found a way to incorporate polemics, madball humor, naturalistic narrative, and his own transforming anger.

In these books, as Bob Skinner observes in *Two Guns from Harlem*, "Himes created a world that was part real and part fantasy and ostensibly used it to entertain. At the same time, he instructed the reader by way of gross exaggeration as to what were the realities of life for the average Black man on the street."

You'll find no simple physical rape in *A Case of Rape*. What you'll find instead is the indictment of far more profound victimizations. Elizabeth Hancock Brissaud is a "casualty of white Christian society," reared to Puritan self-despite and socialized to be forever "feminine," i.e., soft, dependent: a victim. The four accused rapists likewise are victims both of their skin color and their own destructive compulsions.

You'll also find that the trial directs little attention to Elizabeth's death. No one seems much interested in that. It's the matter of her supposed rape by Negroes that takes center stage.

"We are all guilty," the book concludes.

And in that echoing of Dostoevski we confront the range and scope of Himes's intent. For in all his work violence, philosophical issues, questions of culpability, questions of race and sex at the very heart of this culture, commingle.

Here as elsewhere he says that black men, and all women, live permanently exiled from yet surrounded by that culture. That if they are misshapen, monstrous, or pitiful, it's only because they've grown to fit the mold they were formed in.

I could go on to tell you that characters in *A Case of Rape* are modeled on Richard Wright, James Baldwin, William Gardner Smith, cartoonist Ollie Harrington, and Himes himself. To pass along critic Michel Fabre's warning that in attempting to construe the book as a roman a clef (as in so much of Himes's profoundly autobiographical work), you are immediately shunted back from actual events into the world of fiction.

I could go on to point out that, like *The Primitive*, *A Case of Rape* is based on one of Himes's affairs, and direct you to his problematic account of that affair in *The Quality of Hurt*.

But I suspect I've gone on quite long enough.

So let me instead close with a favorite scene from *The Primitive*. Jesse Robinson is yet again chasing the landlord's yippy Pomeranian from his room at a boardinghouse. In the hallway he slips and knocks a white marble nude from its stand. Making a desperate lunge, he catches the statue before it strikes the floor, but falls atop it.

"Good thing you're not in Georgia, son," he says to himself. "Open and shut case of rape."

George Pelecanos
Introduction to *The Big Blowdown*
Introduction by James Sallis

Each moment of our life, each action we take, celebrates both our own uniqueness and the extent to which we manage to abridge that uniqueness in forming connections to others. Similarly, the greatness of any writer may lie in his capacity to confront contradictions within himself : to express among other things, out of the well of his absolute individuality and that of his characters, the many ways in which we are all alike.

Having written that, I peer out into yet another spectacular Arizona sunset (so far away from this world according to Pelecanos), sip coffee, put down my pen.

George Pelecanos now has published seven novels of rare ambition and complexity. And though you are not likely to find him listed among today's hot tickets—on the approved canon of properly serious young writers, say, or in line for foundation grants—he is among the finest ten or twelve novelists working in the U.S. today. So what do I say here? I've been given a bean-shooter, six hundred words, to stand against a lion.

Do I write about the Pelecanos who started off playing such games with conventions of the detective genre, wearing them inside out, sleeves ripped off, nothing underneath? Or the one who wrote a lean, classically noir book just to see if he could do it? About the dedicated chronicler of inner-city Washington, D.C.? The Balzacian figure so intent upon rendering this nation's whole ramshackle , impossible urban life over the past half-century?

Or about how all these are curiously one?

I recall, some years back, the much-trumpeted arrival of a new novel from one of our "A" list writers, and a single calm voice floating to the surface. By book's end, this reviewer said, the protagonist's self-absorption and self-pity, his fear that any break in the day's routine could lead to unspeakable dread from which he'd never recover, may well come to seem like the American experience, rather than the circumscribed experience of the white suburban male; maybe nobody more than a provided-for white guy could be so certain that his crises were those of the world.

It's not a charge ever likely to be leveled on George Pelecanos as he goes quietly about his work.

He writes of immigrants, of blacks, of the young, of all the damaged and disadvantaged and discarded shut away in rented rooms or shuttled aside into bars and diners reeking of stagnant time till, their moment come round at last, they erupt, burn furiously, and expire.

He works hard and shows a rare dedication to that work, continuing with each book to go after what eluded him, what he may have missed the last time out, writing, through the lives of some of its meanest citizens, the whole history of this strange new land, this America where we have murdered ourselves into democracy. True to self and material, he's burrowed in and found direction in the work itself, letting it grow organically, following where it takes him. He's become, in Isaiah Berlin's phrase, both the fox that knows many things and the hedgehog that knows one thing deeply.

At its heart all art asks the same question: How should we live, and how counter the self-destructive nature of ourselves and our history? And at the heart of each Pelecanos novel, that is the theme.

An old friend, Mike Moorcock, recently wrote me that sometimes these days he feels like Big Mama Thornton at an Elvis retrospective. So it is with George Pelecanos. He's the real thing, a powerful and intensely original writer who calls his own tunes and makes us all, bears and people and, yes (as Flaubert said), sometimes the stars alike, dance to them.

You are about to read *The Big Blowdown*, a novel of rare and spectacular achievement.

Treasure this book and its author.

Jean-Patrick Manchette
from *Web del Sol*
"No Safe Ground"

If they're about anything at all beyond mere entertainment, the arts are about amazement and recognition. Certain work, certain paintings, poems, books or music, seem somehow to be in our blood, braided into the DNA: from the first time we encounter them, we know they're a part of us. That's precisely how I felt when I first heard Mozart's horn concerti and the blues or, years later, Cajun music, or when I fetched up on those first lines of Apollinaire, Cendrars, Queneau.

Asked about my devotion to crime fiction by interviewers or by audience members at speaking engagements, I tell them that's the way crime fiction was for me: a crucial part of my intellectual history, amazingly a *familiar* part, from the moment I first cracked open *The Maltese Falcon*. Then, after blathering on about mysteries being the quintessential urban crime fiction, quoting Nathanael West to the effect that in America the novelist has no need to *prepare* for violence, or citing D.H. Lawrence's observation that Americans have murdered their way into democracy, like any good hunting dog I come to point.

These days, the game in the bush tends to be Jean-Patrick Manchette, whose work finally is becoming available to English-language readers.

Each era, I suspect, fumbles its way to a distinctive popular voice, some form or mode uniquely suited to the time's self-image, deeper need and anxieties. Victorian England had its penny dreadfuls, U.S. lawns in the placcid Fifties sprouted the dark mushrooms of original paperbacks by writers like David Goodis and Jim Thompson. As Geoffrey O'Brien observed in *Hardboiled America: The Lurid Years of Paperbacks*, "These novels, and the covers that illustrate them, speak of the ignoble corners of life beyond the glow of Jane Powell, 'Father Knows Best,' and the healthy, smiling faces in magazines advertising milk or frozen dinners or trips to California."

Increasingly I've come to wonder if the thriller—massive engines set in motion and grinding relentlessly on far beyond our tiny lives and ken, provisional realities imploding page by page, horizontal rather than vertical thrust—may not best define and serve our time.

France, of course, adopted American crime fiction early on, giving the genre a certain literary cache and spilling out to the world at large a defining word, noir, with publication of works by Hammett, Chandler, Himes and their French-born disciples in Gallimard's La Serie Noire. Writers largely forgotten here, Horace McCoy, W.R. Burnett and others, remain well-known there. (My own novels come out, under editorship of the prodigious Patrick Raynal, in Gallimard's somewhat updated La Noire.) In France thrillers are referred to as *polars*. And in France the godfather and wizard of polars is Jean-Patrick Manchette.

Much about Jean-Patrick Manchette seems quintessentially French: the stylish glistening surface of his prose, his objectivist method, his adoption of a "low" art form to embody abstract ideas. Possibly this helps explain his remaining all but wholly unknown, and to this point untranslated, in the U.S. All about Europe, having salvaged the French crime novel from the bog of police procedurals and colorful tales of Pigalle lowlife into which it had sunk, he's a massive figure.

"The crime novel," he claimed, "is the great moral literature of our time"—and set about proving it.

City Lights, having recently inaugurated a line of European novels with Carlo Lucarelli's *Almost Blue*, now offers a fine translation of the first of Manchette's stream of ten great novels, *3 to Kill*, with his last, *The Prone Gunman*, promised for spring. Plans are also in place to publish another fine, heretofore untranslated novelist, Thierry Jonquet.

For Manchette and for the generation of writers who followed him, the crime novel is no mere entertainment, but a means to strip bare and put on exhibit society's failures. Their headlong narratives rip apart all received wisdom, rip through veils of appearance, deceit and manipulation to the greed and violence, both implicit and patent, that furnish the society's true engines.

Coming from the extreme left (he was an advocate of Guy Debord's Situationism), Manchette consistently skewered capitalist society and indicted the media for its emphasis on spectacle. His world view was that of a giant marketplace in which gangs of thugs—be they leftist thugs, terrorist thugs, or socially approved thugs like police and politicians—compete relentlessly, and in which small groups of isolated, alienated individuals desperately go on trying to cling to the flotsam of their lives. He folds quotations, allusions and parodies of literary writers like Baudelaire and Stendahl into his work, alludes constantly to music, painting and philosophy, juxtaposes the vulgar and the precious, jams depictions of quotidian life against scenes of such extreme violence as to call into question the whole of bourgeois—of accepted, apparent—existence.

"He was like an electroshock to the chloroformed country of literature and the French thriller," Jean Francois Gerault observed. (Please take note of that *and*.) Elsewhere Gerault suggested that in his final books Manchette "had reached a formal perfection that was impossible to surpass."

Effectively Manchette's career ran only some eleven years or so. The ten novels were published by Gallimard from 1971–1982. Following this, Manchette worked as a translator (of Ross Thomas, Donald Westlake and Alan Moore among others), as a scenarist for film and TV, as an editor (creating a science fiction series), as reviewer of films and essayist on thrillers and crime fiction. After 1989, treatment of and complications from a pancreatic tumor made work impossible. He died in 1995 in Paris of lung cancer, aged 53.

From the first page of *3 to Kill*, from virtually any page of Manchette, you know right away you're in the hands of a master and reach for something to hold on to, because you also know the ride's going to be wild, hard, and fast.

And sometimes what used to happen was what is happening now: Georges Gerfaut is driving on Paris's outer ring road. He has entered at the Porte d'Ivry. It is two-thirty or maybe three-fifteen in the morning ... He has had five glasses of Four Roses bourbon. And about three hours ago he took two capsules of a powerful barbiturate. The combined effect on him has not been drowsiness but a tense euphoria that threatens at any moment to change into anger or else into a kind of vaguely Chekhovian and essentially bitter melancholy, not a very valiant or interesting feeling …

Georges Gerfaut is a man under forty. His car is a steel-grey Mercedes. The leather upholstery is mohagony brown, matching all the fittings of the vehicle's interior. As for Georges Gerfaut's interior, it is somber and confused....Via two speakers, one beneath the dashboard, the other on the back-window deck, a tape player is quietly diffusing West Coast-style jazz …

The reason why Georges is barreling along the outer ring road, with diminished reflexes, listening to this particular music, must be sought first and foremost in the position occupied by Georges in the social relations of production. The fact that Georges has killed at least two men in the course of the last year is not germane. What is happening now used to happen from time to time in the past.

Never on safe ground with Manchette, as here we're always more or less off kilter and balance, sometimes unsure just where in the story we are—in medias res, flashback, trapped in some sort of eternal recurrence?

Stopping to aid a severely injured man, Gerfaut attracts the attention of the man's attackers. They set themselves then on Gerfaut who, failing to connect the two occurrences and with no idea what is going on, nonetheless steps aside, out of his own life, to turn the killing back on them. It's a standard thriller plot, the pursued becoming pursuer; the amazement is in seeing how much of the world Manchette effortlessly loops and lassos into his novel as scenes, situations and confrontations pour out like frosted breath on a cold morning.

Manchette's are lean, muscular books that deserve serious reading. In this age of hyperbole and unremitting puffery, they have the uncommon decency and grace to appear much simpler than they are: to mean much more than they say.

Jean-Patrick Manchette
Introduction for *The Mad and the Bad*
New York Review Books
Introduction by James Sallis

In America it was Hammett and Chandler. Hammett who took murder out of the manor houses and gave it back to the people who actually commit it. Chandler who fashioned of bus stations, diners and cheap hotel rooms, at the frontier's last raw edge, a mythology specifically American. In France the new maps were drawn by Jean-Patrick Manchette.

When Manchette began to write his novels in the mid-1970s, the French *polar* had become a still pool of police procedurals and tales of Pigalle lowlife. Manchette wanted to throw in rocks, disturb the calm surface, bring up all the muck beneath—to demonstrate that the crime novel could be (as he said again and again) "the great moral literature of our time."

For Manchette and the generation of writers who succeeded him, then, these novels became far more than simple entertainment; they became a means of facing society's failures head on. One after another the curtains will be torn back. Pretense. Deceit. Manipulation. Till there in the small, choked room behind it all we witness society's true engines—greed and violence—grinding away.

"He was like an electroshock to the chloroformed country of literature and the French thriller," Jean-Francois Gerault noted.

Manchette published ten novels with Gallimard from 1971–1982. Before and after, he worked as an editor, reviewed movies, wrote scripts for film and TV and numerous essays on thrillers and crime fiction. He also published translations of Ross Thomas, Donald Westlake, Alan Moore and others—at least thirty books. By 1989, treatment of and complications from a pancreatic tumor made work difficult. He died in 1995 in Paris of lung cancer, aged 53, before completing a new novel, *La Princesse du sang* (*Princess of the Blood*), intended to be the first of a five-book cycle covering five decades from the post-war period to the present.

The Mad and the Bad, original title *Ô dingos,Ô châteaux!*, came early in the game, in 1972, following close upon the prior year's collaborative *Laissez bronzer les Cadavres* (*Corpses in the Sun*, with Jean-Pierre Bastid) and solo *L'Affaire N'Gustro* (*The N'Gustro Affair*), winning that year's grand prize for crime fiction.

The novel's tale of a young woman and boy set upon by deadly forces beyond their understanding shows the co-opting of classic noir plots we see in all Manchette's novels. In *3 to Kill* a businessman witnesses a murder and, pursued by the killers, steps away from his ordinary life to turn the killing back on them. In *The Prone Gunman* a hired killer yearning to give it all up returns catastrophically to his hometown. The pleasure lies in the many ways Manchette twists and turns his story on the spit of plot, how he transforms the expected, how much weight he manages to pack into scenes that remain lean and muscular. Things move fast, almost at a blur—then excruciatingly slow. Sentences are clipped, headlong. Charged language everywhere, sometimes to the point of the incantory.

Here also are Manchette's trademark disavowed individuals, ill-fitting stones in societal walls that will crumble at the first wayward blow.

"The nursemaid before you. Completely off her rocker. Fifty if she was a day. And an idiot. What about you? What's your thing?"

"I don't understand at all," said Julie. "My thing? What do you mean?"

"The thing that's screwy with you."

"I'm cured," Julie stated.

"The hell you are!" exclaimed the driver." The boss's way of doing good is over the top. He only hires retards. He sets up factories for cripples to work in, can you figure that?"

"Not really."

"Those guys who go around in little motorized wheelchairs? He's got them working on a production line! In this house it's the same baloney. The cook is epileptic. The gardener has only one arm, pretty handy for using the shears. His private secretary is blind. His valet suffers from locomotor ataxia—no wonder his meals arrive cold! The snotty brat's old nanny—well, I told you about her. As for you, you must know yourself."

"What about you?" asked Julie.

She had taken out a pack of Gauloises and a Criquet lighter. She lit a cigarette and, throwing her head back, blew smoke through her nostrils.

"What about you?" she repeated.

A parade of grotesquerie, dialogue rich in subtext, and a parody of labor in capitalist society—all in less than a page.

There's much that's quintessentially French about Manchette: his political stance, the stylish hard surface of his prose, his adoption of a "low" or demotic art form to embody abstract ideas. Like any great illusionist, he directs our attention one way as the miraculous happens another. He tells us a simple story. This occurred. That. But there's bone, there's gristle. Floors give way, and wind heaves its shoulder against the door. His stories of cornered individuals become an indictment of capitalism's excesses, its unchallenged power, its reliance on distraction and spectacle.

For Manchette the world is a giant marketplace in which gangs of thugs—be they leftist, reactionary, terrorist, police or politicians—compete relentlessly; one in which tiny groups of individuals, "torn to pieces by the enemy and sodomized by [their] own leaders," stay afloat by clinging to the flotsam. In his work he alludes to and parodies literary writers such as Baudelaire and Stendahl, juxtaposes the vulgar and the precious, enjambs depictions of quotidian life against scenes of such extreme and often implicit violence as to call into question all the myriad fictions of bourgeois, accepted existence. Like Hammett he affirms that everyone lies; like Rimbaud, that everything we are taught is false.

Manchette revered Chandler and Hammett as founders of the form in which he worked, and in Chandler's lyrical description from "The Simple Art of Murder" found a world he well recognized.

The realist in murder writes of a world in which gangsters can rule nations and almost rule cities, in which hotels and apartment houses and celebrated restaurants are owned by men who made their money out of brothels, in which a screen star can be the fingerman for a mob, and the nice man down the hall is a boss of the numbers racket; a world where a judge with a cellar full of bootleg liquor can send a man to jail for having a pint in his pocket, where the mayor of your town may have condoned murder as an instrument of moneymaking, where no man can walk down a dark street in safety because law and order are things we talk about but refrain from practising ...

It is not a very fragrant world, but it is the world you live in, and certain writers with tough minds and a cool spirit of detachment can make very interesting and even amusing patterns out of it. It is not funny that a man should be killed, but it is sometimes funny that he should be killed for so little, and that his death should be the coin of what we call civilization.

Though dredged from the same dark well of purloined promise as Chandler's, Manchette's profoundly leftist, distinctly European stance may be something of a problem for American readers. Like many of his generation, Manchette was influenced by the Situationist Guy Debord, whose theories, elaborated in *The Society of the Spectacle*, were everywhere during France's 1968 insurrections. Situationists held that capitalism's overweening successes came only at the expense of increased alienation, social dysfunction and a general degradation of daily life; that the acquisition, exchange and consumption of commodities had forcefully supplanted direct experience, creating a kind of life by proxy; and that liberation might be found in fashioning moments that reawakened authentic desires, a sense of adventure, a ransom from dailyness.

Again and again one finds similar ideas in Manchette, here as a loose scaffolding holding story parts together, there like bones poking through broken skin. Manchette's stories clip along at breakneck speed, breath be damned, skimming over polarized societies and forfeited lives, momentum never flagging. And in that disjunction, lightness of surface supporting the heaviness beneath, Manchette found his voice.

Back in the hills of the rural South where I grew up, squirrel hunters often nailed their game to trees and, with a knife and brute strength, tore the body from the skin in a single hard pull. As a method it was clean, quick, and efficient. The skins stayed behind on the trees, dozens of them, all around cabins and favorite hunting sites, constant reminders.

Books like Manchette's are those skins.

Boris Vian
Introduction to *I'll Spit on Your Graves*
Canonogate Books (UK)
"Bussing the Lips of the Grave"
by James Sallis

I don't want to die, he wrote in one of his poems, till I've known the black dogs of Mexico who sleep without dreams, till I've seen bare-assed apes devouring the tropics, silver spiders in their nests sewn of bubbles. I don't want to die till I've savoured the taste of death.

That dark, acrid taste flowered in his mouth on June 23, 1959, as he sat watching the screening of the film made from a novel he'd written under a pseudonym and put forth to the world as a translation—the very novel you hold in your hands. A heart damaged in youth and pushed for too long too far past its limits at last let go. He was 39 years old, as "the Prince of Saint-Germain" one of Paris's most visible man: poet, jazz trumpeter and writer on jazz, songwriter and chanteur, translator, playwright, failed novelist. He was Boris Vian.

It was as translator that he presented *J'Irai cracher sur vos tombes*, purportedly the work of an American black, Vernon Sullivan, "whom no American editor dared publish," to French readers. He'd written it himself, on a bet with wife Michelle and publisher Jean d'Halluin of Editions du Scorpion, in two weeks while on vacation with his family. During a discussion of current

141

books, Vian exclaimed: "A best seller? Give me ten days and I'll make you one!" His bluff was called.

Vian at the time had no way of knowing how thoroughgoing would be that hastily-midwifed book's influence upon his life. Published in 1946, a bestseller in 1947, with sales in advance of half a million by 1950, the book became hugely important in allowing him to withdraw from employ as an engineer and devote his time to writing. Also as a direct result of this mock translation, Vian received a contract to translate Kenneth Fearing's *The Big Clock*; renderings of novels by James M. Cain and science fiction writer A.E. Van Vogt, General Omar Bradley's *History of a Soldier*, and, most notably, Chandler's *The Lady in the Lake* and *The Big Sleep*, followed. There'd be three further "Sullivan" novels as well. All positive consequences, true enough—but publication of *J'Irai cracher* would also immure Vian in years of litigation. This began in February 1947 when self-appointed public watchdog Daniel Parker sponsored a lawsuit against the novel. (Vian had his small revenge in naming the murderer-protagonist of his second Sullivan novel after Parker.) Shortly thereafter, in a cheap motel room in Montparnasse, a man strangled his mistress to death. A copy of Vian/Sullivan's novel, like a devotional or pillow book, stood at bedside. The passage in which Lee Anderson strangles Jean Asquit, among others, was circled.

> She lay there on the ground, with her eyes closed and her skirt pushed up on her belly. I again felt that strange sensation that ran up my back and my hand closed on her throat and I couldn't stop myself; it came; it was so strong that I let her go and almost staggered to my feet.

Sales of the novel burgeoned. By 1949 the French government had officially banned the book. And in 1951, at the end of a string of court appearances during which he finally admitted authorship, Vian was fined 100,000 francs.

Another unsuspected consequence was that Vian's own work fell to the shadow of Sullivan's notoriety. Three years after Vian's death, with half a million copies of *J'Irai cracher* sold, Gallimard still retained in its warehouse over a third of its run (1,250 copies of 4,400) of Vian's extraordinary novel *L'Ecume des jours*, published in the year of Sullivan's peak sales, 1947. Vian's first novel, *Vercoquin et le plancton*, and *L'Automne à Pékin* (which came out alongside *L'Ecume* in 1947) proved just as unsuccessful. A follow-up Sullivan novel, *Les Morts ont tous la meme peau*, also emerged in 1947. It fared somewhat, though not spectacularly, better.

France and Paris especially, recall, had just emerged from German occupation and Vichy repression. Parisians sought out casual pleasures: parties, café life, music, drink. A cult of youth stalked the land; there was a general loosening of sexual taboos and an infatuation not only with jazz and the Negroes who created it, but with all things American. Gallimard's La Série Noire reflected the French fascination with American thrillers. Sartre, that perennial champion of engaged writers, sailed off to the Orient of New York City to return with holds full of contracts for books by American novelists.

In *Difficult Lives,* my study of Fifties paperback writers, I noted: "It's not difficult to see how postwar French readers came across books like these with a certain shock of recognition. The lack of meaning in it all, the way events just happen—that zero at the center—was very much in the air, simmering into existentialism on Left Bank stoves. In American hardboiled writing, French readers found something both of the intense isolation and anxiety of writers like Gide and Malraux and of the stylistic qualities they so admired (and admire still) in Faulkner, Hemingway, Steinbeck and Caldwell.

"The French in fact recognized what no American critic at the time perceived: that stripped-down novels like those of McCoy, Cain or Goodis, trembling on the very edge of the real, all but canceling themselves out in their starkness, were something new, achieving a penetration, a depth, not possible with earlier narrative modes. France's greatest homage to this new fiction, and one of the great modern novels, came in 1942, seven years after publication of *They Shoot Horses*, with Camus' *The Stranger*."

French readers too, like their U.S. counterparts among urban intellectuals, had a fixation with American racial problems. French newspapers routinely ran articles on lynchings in Southern states, Sartre sponsored a series on U.S. race relations in the hugely influential *Les Temps modernes*, his popular play *La Putain respectueuse* confronted the problem head-on.

That morning of June 23, 1959, as Boris Vian sank into his seat at the Cinema Marbeuf to preview the film of *J'Irai*, as devotee of jazz, as translator of American hardboiled fiction, as contributor to

Les Temps modernes, he was well aware of all this; these strains were everywhere about him, bearing him up. That morning, he had neglected to take his heart medications. Some time back, appalled at the direction the film adaptation had taken, he had demanded that his name be expunged from the credits. Now as the first frames ticked by onscreen, he spoke up: "These guys are supposed to be American? my ass!" Then he collapsed. Shortly thereafter, he was declared dead.

Life on its own, as fervently and as furiously as he embraced it, had never been quite enough for Boris Vian. It needed always the seasoning of imagination: rhetorical figures, filigrees of language, talismans of the everyday turned back on themselves, metempsychoses of word and world, a touch of the mythic.

In the Avant Propos to *L'Ecume des jours* he had written:

> "There are only two things: love, all sorts of love, with pretty girls, and the music of New Orleans or Duke Ellington. Everything else ought to go, because everything else is ugly, and the few pages of proof which follow derive all their strength from the fact that this is a completely true story, since I imagined it from start to finish."

The Imagination is not a State, William Blake wrote, it is the Human Existence itself.

• • •

Typically, in setting out to write an American thriller Boris Vian ignored unlocked front doors and walked past back gates left off the latch and ajar. He went in, instead, through the bedroom window.

J'Irai cracher sur vos tombes—*I'll Spit on Your Graves*—resembles nothing so much as a line of funhouse mirrors in which, at first mildly distorting, amusing, the figure grows increasingly more grotesque as one moves along.

Mirrors, too, because here we have a white man (Vian) pretending to be a black man (Sullivan) writing a novel about a black man (Lee Anderson) pretending to be white.

In the second novel "Sullivan" plays it out even further. Dan Parker leads a good, uncomplicated life until one day he's approached by a black half-brother who threatens to put it about that Parker is partially black. Continuing the theme of skewed representation, mirrors within mirrors, this claim is untrue, but before Parker can unfold the lie he has lost all sense of self, of identity. He becomes a murderer, then, in the unfolding's wake, a suicide.

> Dan appeared to come out from a dream. With a slow, inexorable gesture, he climbed on the window's ledge and bent in order to be able to jump. He noticed below, far away on the road, a compact group of people and, instinctively, he maneuvered his body in order to avoid them. He turned in the air like a clumsy frog and crashed on the hard surface of the street.

Mirrors might serve as metaphor of Vian's method, too, as he turns thriller conventions back on themselves and lets them feed, cranking everything up notch by notch, spooling out what Bart Plantenga has called "a pastiche of jokes, clunky B-movie tropes, sex, puns and send-ups," as though to see just how far he can go, just how much he can get away with—like Lee Anderson.

Vian's description of principles in the Avant Propos for *L'Ecume des jours* not only seems appropriate here but also remains one of the finest evocations of the creative process I know.

> Properly speaking, its method consists in projecting reality, under favorable circumstances, onto an irregularly tilting and consequently distorting frame of reference. As you can see, if ever there was a procedure that does us credit, this is it.

Passing for white, Lee like a latter-day Pied Piper seduces the town's youth with liquor, sexuality and guitar playing, comforming to the very stereotype of the dangerous black man. Hit the brakes again and turn. Vian's nihilism and misanthropy, this dashed-off essay on man's corrupt being that is *I'll Spit on Your Graves*, becomes finally a kind of inverted idealism. And yes, though in Bart Plantenga's words it "borders on trash while fondling literature and winking at pornography," it does us credit.

• • •

Celebrated in *Vercoquin et le plancton* and *Trouble dans les Andains*, zazous were an underground cultural resistance to German occupation, youth groups ignoring realities of the political situation to pursue surprise parties, outrageous pranks, American jazz, arcane culture, obscure art—to pitch tents of irony and rebellion and deliver to the culture at large (please sign here to acknowledge receipt) youth's eternal raspberry. Outriders held strong attraction for Vian; a lifelong devotee of science fiction and other marginal literatures, he burrowed hedgehoglike into the secret life of black jazzmen, later became a satrap—a kind of guru sans portfolio, but with clown hat provided—in the College of Pataphysics. ("Only the College of Pataphysics does not undertake to save the world.") Just as he took his measure of most things, Vian had his own reading, too, of *engagé*. Uncommitted to Sartrean gospel, that gospel he lampoons so affectionately in *L'Ecume des jours*, Vian is nonetheless committed: to exemption, to exception, to the comic, weird and miraculous.

Inasmuch as it fosters any intellectual climate at all, society today fosters one extolling opposition and hostility to the norm as the only honorable, ethical stand towards it. Nostalgia plays a part here. Surely there was an Eden, something we've lost or been exiled from, some time and place when all made sense, to which we must find our way back. Or, looking through from the other side, surely it's imperative that we reject received wisdom, toss overboard all those things we so smugly "know," strike out for new sensations, new territories, new understandings.

Vian was one of the great iconoclasts, just as in our youth we're all great iconoclasts, anti-cleric, anti-military, opposed to society's workaday accommodations. Often, indeed, Vian's seems the very literature of perpetual youth: brash and unabashedly disrespectful, locked into an eternal, egoistic present, lacking in acknowledgment of (or for that matter, knowledge of) achievements of the past. The adolescent is forever sundered, alone, forever striking out against a world which fails again and yet again to be the one he was promised, the one he's still told, day after day and in a thousand dishonest ways, it is. Shut under this lid of discontent, idealism simmers to a bitter, thick stew.

In *L'Ecume des jours*, Colin's girlfriend Chloe dies of a flower growing in her lung. Here is Colin upon her death.

> He raised his eyes and saw Jesus hanging on his cross above the altar-rail in front of him. He looked fed up and Colin said to him, "Why did Chloe have to die?"

"Nothing to do with me," said Jesus. "It's not my responsibility. Let's talk about something else ..."

"Whose responsibility is it then?" asked Colin.

They talked together quietly and the others could not hear what they were saying.

"Not mine, at any rate," said Jesus.

"I did ask you to my wedding," said Colin.

"That was fun," said Jesus. "I had a smashing time."

...

He looked somewhere else and seemed bored again. Father Phigga swung a rattle while shouting a Latin chorus.

"Why did you make her die?" asked Colin.

"Oh! ..." said Jesus. "Shut up."

He wriggled to get more comfortable on his nails.

"She was so sweet," said Colin. "She never did anything bad—and she never had an evil thought."

"That's nothing to do with religion," mumbled Jesus with a yawn.

He shook his head to the other side to change the angle of his crown of thorns.

"I don't know what we did to deserve this," said Colin.

He lowered his eyes. Jesus did not reply. Colin raised his head. Jesus' chest was going gently up and down. His features were smooth and calm. His eyes were closed and Colin could hear a soft smug purring sound coming from his nostrils like an overfed cat.

In Vian's world, because the people they loved are gone, mice persuade diffident cats to kill them, and stallions are crucified for their supposed sins. Children, when they begin to stray, are shut into cages. Sunlight, scarves, walls, bathroom fixtures—all these have an existence of their own, one quite independent of mankind's. Just as Colin has taken on faith everything told him, so does the world become literal; as though in illustration of Wittgenstein, world equals word. When Colin puts on Duke Ellington's "The Mood to Be Wooed," the o's on the record label cause the corners of the room to become round. As Chloe weakens, her bed sinks closer and closer to the ground and the room grows ever smaller. At her funeral, since Colin has no more money, her coffin is simply thrown out the window, breaking the leg of a child playing in the gutter below.

• • •

Much of Vian's work remains untranslated. To date, aside from the novel you hold, only *L'Ecume des jours* (*Froth on the Daydream* in Stanley Chapman's translation, *Mood Indigo* in John Sturrock's), *L'Arrache-coeur* (*Heartsnatcher*, again translated by Chapman), and a single collection of stories (*Blues for a Black Cat*, translated from *Les Fourmis* by Julia Older) are available. Two other fine novels, the expansive *L'Automne à Pékin* and the brief, intense *L'Herbe rouge*, should long past have made their way into English. *[Note: They now have.]*

In the latter novel, Wolf invents a time machine. Haunted by memories and by the ravages of childhood, he hopes the machine will deliver him from the past; instead it delivers him ever more surely and inescapably *to* the past.

This becomes a familiar theme with Vian, this crashing of the past onto the present's shores, leaving his characters shipwrecked there. Vian's own childhood illness reaches forward over the years to claim him, not only physically (the damaged heart, however ignored, at last closing like a fist about his life) but in more pervasive ways as well—just as Wolf's memories overtake him. The children of *L'Arrache-coeur*, bound to their mother's insecurities, fitted with steel boots and finally placed in cages, reflect Vian's own sense of maternal smothering as a child forbidden, because of his illness, ordinary activity. Also in *L'Arrache-çoeur*, Jacquemort must fish the refuse of an entire village—its guilt—from the river with his teeth. In Vian's play *Les Bâtisseurs d'Empire* (*The Empire Builders*) a mysterious, unspeaking, mummylike figure pursues a family inexorably from home to home, room to room, floor to floor.

And in the case of Lee Anderson herewith, even as he tries to escape his past by direct action, to bring it to some level, that past overtakes and destroys him.

In 1962 Jean-Jacques Pauvert brought out, under the title *Je voudrais pas crever*, a collection of Vian's best poems. The first of these, in which Vian sketches out the scope and wonder of life remaining to be seen, to be experienced, you read in part back at the beginning of this introduction. In the collection's final poem, "Je mourrai d'un cancer de la colonne vertébrale," Vian imagines the experience of his death. He will die from spinal cancer, from injuries incurred when a giant rat springs from its lair to tear away an arm, under the sun with eyelids cut away, of drowning or in fire, of having watched the torture of children; he'll be crushed by the sky when it falls. He will die, he says, a little, a lot, watching with great interest.

And then, when all that's done with, he will die.

At age 39—though he did not know this—as lights go down and imitations of life, imitations *of* imitations, pale as his own failing life, roll up onscreen.

Boris Vian
Review of *The Dead All Have the Same Skin*
TamTam Books, Trans. Paul Knobloch
For the *LA Times*
by James Sallis

Imagine an intellectual, astutely French, who hangs out with the likes of Jean-Paul Sarte, has a child's sense of humor and of the world's newness, writes radically perverse novels and spends his evenings playing trumpet with jazz bands 'round about the Left Bank. There you pretty much have Boris Vian.

Life on its own, however fervently and furiously embraced, was never enough for him. It needed the seasoning of imagination: rhetorical figures, filigrees of language, slapstick, turns of phrase and radical shifts of perspective, a touch of the mythic, a pinch of the mystic. He'd walk by front doors left ajar, squeeze his way in through a basement window propped half open.

In an early story about the Normandy invasion Vian wrote: "We arrived this morning and weren't well received. No one was on the beach but a lot of dead guys (or pieces of dead guys), tanks, and demolished trucks. Bullets flew from almost everywhere ... The boy just behind me had three-quarters of his face removed by a whizzing bullet. I put the pieces in my helmet and gave them to him."

Of the dead-unserious group in which he was central, he remarked, "Only the College of Pataphysicians does not undertake to save the world." Asked to fill out a form in triplicate, Vian said, the Pataphysician will remove the carbons and enter different information on each sheet. That playfulness and refusal to be pinned down peeks out, Kilroy-like, from all that Vian wrote.

His great novel, *L'Écume des jours* (*Foam of the Daze*), is a tragedy of young love in which a woman dies of the lily growing in her lung. As she worsens, her bed sinks closer and closer to the floor and the room grows ever smaller. In Vian's world, because the people they loved are gone, mice persuade diffident cats to kill them. Stallions are crucified for their sins. Children, when they stray—as in *L'Arrache-coeur* (*Heartsnatcher*)—are shut into cages. Bells detach themselves from doors to come and announce visitors; neckties rebel against being knotted; some broken windowpanes grow back overnight, while others darken from breathing difficulties; armchairs and sausages must be calmed before use. When Colin, of *L'Écume*, puts Duke Ellington's "The Mood to Be Wooed" on the phonograph, the O's on the record label cause the corners of the room to become round.

Vian died in 1959, at 39, while watching the screening of a film made from *J'Irai cracher sur vos tombes* (*I Spit on Your Graves*), a 1946 novel he wrote under the pseudonym Vernon Sullivan and put out as a translation. A bestseller in France, it became also a cause célèbre and the subject of litigation when a man strangled his mistress to death in a Montmartre motel, leaving behind a copy of the novel with violent passages marked. That novel, published in 1998 by TamTam, is the story of a black man who passes for white in a Southern town in order to avenge the lynching of his brother by courting and killing two white sisters.

The Dead All Have the Same Skin is, if not literally, then spiritually, a sequel. Vian wrote two further Vernon Sullivan novels, in which he kicked out all the stops and skidded toward parody; neither has the authority or purchase of the first two. Reminiscent of Chester Himes' sadly neglected *Run Man Run* in its intensity and its protagonist's needless headlong rush to oblivion, *The Dead All Have the Same Skin* also verges—with its fierce energy, candor and matter-of-fact savagery—on Jim Thompson territory: "I liked it. I got a kick out of pummeling the heads of those pigs. But after five years I've started to lose my taste for this particular sport. Five years and not a soul suspects it. No one has the slightest idea that a man of mixed blood, a colored man, has been the one pounding on their heads each and every night."

Dan Parker works as a bouncer in a New York club. It's all gone stale: drunken clients, available women, the buzz of violence, the hard-and-easy sex. Living as white in a white world, he has always felt out of place and vaguely afraid, but he has his home, his white wife and kid, his job. And when braced by Richard, a black man claiming to be his brother, Dan fears it will all come undone. From that moment, we are securely in the jaws of classic noir, as, driven by circumstance, careening from one dreadful act to another, Dan becomes his own chatty tour guide to damnation.

If only …

But character is destiny and writes the script of our lives.

"I killed Richard for nothing. His bones snapped under the force of my hands. I killed the girl with one punch. And now the pawnbroker is dead, again for no reason … I killed them all for absolutely no reason. And now I've lost Sheila and the hotel is being surrounded."

The Dead All Have the Same Skin came out in 1947, at the peak of success for *I Spit on Your Graves*. These years were signal for Vian, seeing, along with the two Sullivan novels, the novels *Vercoquin et le plancton*, *L'automne à Pékin* and *L'Écume des jours*. *L'Herbe rouge* (1950) and *L'Arrache-coeur* (1953) followed, but none managed to match the triumph of the first Sullivan book. (When he died, Gallimard had more than 1,250 of the 4,400-copy run of *L'Écume* warehoused.)

In ensuing years, Vian's career skittered. He turned to translation, rendering into French novels by Kenneth Fearing and James M. Cain, as well as Raymond Chandler's *The Lady in the Lake* and *The Big Sleep*. He wrote plays, such as *The Empire Builders* and *The General's Tea Party*. He published poetry and numerous articles, many of these springing from, and reflecting, his pedigree as Pataphysician. He performed and recorded original songs, again achieving notoriety with his take on the Algerian war in "Le Déserteur." He wrote on jazz for *Combat* and other publications, these pieces latterly collected as *Round About Close to Midnight: The Jazz Writings of Boris Vian*.

Certainly, Vian is not to every taste. As is said of pulp fiction, there's much silliness mixed in with the driven, hard-edged storytelling. Ever the iconoclast and reconstructed adolescent, Vian continually pushes boundaries and crawls under barricades, seeing how much he can get away with. Yet like other great arealist writers, he had a way of dipping into the pools of archetypes and primal emotions we all share—very much, in fact, like Jacquemort, of *L'Arrache-coeur*, condemned to fish the refuse of an entire village, all of its guilt, from the river with his teeth.

In recent years, L.A.-based publisher TamTam Books has given us an exemplary new translation of *L'Écume des jours*, a new edition of *I Spit on Your Graves* and the first English translation of *L'Automne à Pékin*. Now TamTam, much to be commended, midwives this outstanding translation by Paul Knobloch, with a third Vernon Sullivan novel promised.

Gerald Kersh
For the program book *Readercon 1999*
"Feverish Country, This"
by James Sallis

In *I Got References,* the collection of stories, sketches and autobiographical snippets that Paul Duncan says may be the closest we'll ever come as readers to sitting down for a chat with its author, Gerald Kersh writes of his devil-take-the-hindmost childhood.

> I achieved notoriety on account of my destructive tendencies. Once, when a tramcar fell over near Acton, I was seized and chastised, as it were absent-mindedly, as soon as the crash was heard.

This shows, I think, something both of the man's intense egoism and of his native skill as raconteur. In many ways Kersh continued all his life to be the bad boy of literature. Born early into the new century, some eight years before (as Virginia Woolf has it) human nature changed utterly, he rode in on the last hurrahs of several grand British literary traditions, freelancing articles and sketches to the *Daily Mirror* and *London Evening Standard* in Fleet Street, publishing short stories in the many newspapers and magazines for which they were then a mainstay. This was the heyday of the short story, in fact, and high-circulation, high-profile magazines like *Collier's* and *the Saturday Evening Post* and their counterparts in the UK could provide a fine living. Demand, both there and at lower-paying markets such as *John O'London's Weekly* or the pulps that specialized in various forms of romance and adventure, was high; many writers specialized, turning out stories by the dozen and little else. Modernism might have been busily kicking over the traces elsewhere, but here standards remained deeply rooted in nineteenth-century notions of popular literature and the well-made story. Nor, again as in 19th-century writing, had "unnatural" elements been purged, as shortly they would be, in favor of a thoroughgoing realism. Magazines offered up heady blends of exoticism, sea adventures, Wellsian science fiction and moral tales, ghost stories, crime stories.

Here in the States, it's mostly for his stories, of which he wrote several hundred, that Kersh is remembered when he is known at all. Many of these, though generally given his distinctive stamp, were staple fare for magazine writers of the time: ventriloquist's dummy stories ("The Extraordinarily Horrible Dummy"), Siamese twins stories ("The Sympathetic Souse"), cursed- jewel stories ("Seed of Destruction"), circus- or carnival-folk stories ("The Queen of Pig Island"), stories of possession ("The Eye" and, again, "The Extraordinarily Horrible Dummy"). These might in fact more properly be called tales. The majority have elements of the fantastic; if not of the fantastic, then of the grotesque. Many are built around some central gimmick—what if one Siamese twin were a drunk, the other a teetotaler, for instance—and have a trick or reverse ending, some final revelation that snaps the tale into new focus.

They share, too, another strategy common to older work. Many are framed, i.e., presented to the reader as true stories garnered from obscure documents (the last days of Ambrose Bierce in "The Oxoxoco Bottle"), come upon in journals (a Japanese man thrown back in time by detonation of the bomb over Hiroshima in "The Brighton Monster"), or overheard from others (the truly nightmarish creatures of "Men Without Bones"). Kersh from time to time even steps directly into the doorway of the story, presenting himself under his own name as interlocutor. This convention has the dual purpose of lending formal credibility to a story's events and, by placing fantastical or highly-charged events at a remove, of softening and safening them—taming the story's savage heart.

History, the shadow of great events, also looms over Kersh's stories— Hiroshima in "The Brighton Monster," the Cold War in "Prophet

Without Honor," the Balkans in "Reflections in a Tablespoon," slavery in "Fantasy of a Hunted Man"—perhaps as another way of cranking up wattage, raising the game's stakes. Kersh was, after all, competing vigorously and continuously with hundreds of others for the reader's (and editor's) attention.

As a short story writer Kersh largely belongs to that group of writers Anthony Burgess characterized as making literature from the intrusion of fantasy or horror into a real world closely observed. Their tales more often suggest fable or a sort of grand guignol than the plodding naturalism of much modern work, Burgess notes. They are likely to ransack traditions but not to belong, themselves, to any tradition. And while themselves quite "literary," they play no part in the development of literature: even the most comprehensive histories of English-language literature have no room at the inn for the likes of Saki, John Collier, Mervyn Peake, or Gerald Kersh. This is a type of writer rarely seen today—a type already fading during Kersh's time.

If Kersh's approach at times could be indirect or sidling ("I had this curious story from a gentlemen in the Paradise Bar ..."), his engagement with the material was not. One early critic termed his stories "frontal assaults." Not uncommonly do we come upon such arresting descriptions as that of the wasted, drunken beauty whose eyes have become like "a couple of cockroaches desperately swimming in two saucers of boiled rhubarb," or of the divan whose springs protrude "like the entrails of a disembowelled horse." Nor are Kersh's people often of the nicest sort; he himself spoke of them as having been "quarried" rather than born.

Yet Burgess proclaimed Sam Yudenow from *Fowler's End* a comic character on the order of Falstaff. In *The Thousand Deaths of Mr. Small*, another reviewer asserted, Kersh had created " a character capable of standing on its own feet beside Wilkins Micawber." Harry Fabian of *Night and the City* intrigues us still, sixty years after he first swam into our ken, as do the va-et-vients and divagations of Busto's rooming-house in *The Song of a Flea*. And if at first we read for the outrageous stories and sometimes still more outrageous characters, we reread (and Kersh readers one and all, I have found, are veteran rereaders) for quite different reasons: marvelous evocations of down-and-out London; discursions that springboard off some passing observation and continue on marvelously for page after page, pushing all else for the moment aside; startling felicities of language that seem to appear fullblown from nowhere, as though the sentences themselves had burst into flame.

Harlan Ellison, in his introduction to *Nightshades and Damnations*, offered up a few notes from Kersh's Greatest Hits.

> We hang about the necks of our tomorrows like hungry harlots about the necks of penniless sailors.

> A storm broke, and at every clap of thunder the whole black sky splintered like a window struck by a bullet—starred and cracked in ten thousand directions letting in flashes of dazzling light ...

> ... there are men whom one hates until a certain moment when one sees, through a chink in their armor, the writhing of something nailed down and in torment.

Harlan and I alike admire Kersh's description of a man so characterless as to be all but nonexistent, whose tie is "patterned with dots like confetti trodden into the dust" and whose "oddment of limp brownish mustache resembled a cigarette-butt, disintegrating shred by shred in a tea-saucer."

Kersh is a master of metaphor in a manner rare among novelists, lashing whole chapters, the creation of entire characters and vibrant scenes, to the scaffolding of what are essentially extended metaphors. Here, for example, is his stunning portrait of a married couple in *Fowler's End*, that sinkhole purlieu of London you find by "going northward, step by step, into the neighborhoods that most strongly repel you."

> He was a quick, hideously ugly little man, cold and viscous about the hands, with a gecko's knack of sticking to plane surfaces. Once, when I went into his shop to buy a handkerchief, Godbolt, telling me that he didn't have much call for that kind of thing nowadays but thought he had a few in stock, went to get one from a high shelf. It may have been the effect of the fog but I will swear I saw him run up the wall. He had a black-cotton fly of a wife who was always buzzing at him from a distance; she never came within less than five feet of him—for

fear, presumably, that he might thrust out a glutinous green tongue and catch her. He was always watching her out of the corners of his horny-lidded, protruberant eyes.

I've slipped here, you'll note, from speaking of Kersh as a short-story writer to speaking of him as a novelist. There's a considerable divorce between the two, and for all his facility as a story writer, for all his touches of the grotesque and fantastic therein, it's in the novel, and as a realist, that his specific genius found full force and strength. Stories often seem to have been taken up rather light-heartedly, perhaps chiefly as a means to pay rent or provide passage for yet another relocation, turned out quickly, one suspects, and sent off virtually as the last page emerged from the typewriter. The novels he appears to have taken more seriously. Again, it is 19th-century models, Kipling early on, Dickens a bit later, to which they invite comparison.

While publication of his third novel, *Night and the City*, in 1938 brought major attention, it was as a war novelist that Kersh first began earning significant money from his writing and became well known. In these novels he showed a naturalist, almost taxidermic slant quite in contrast to the exoticism and fantastic elements of his short stories.

1942 *They Died With Their Boots Clean*
1942 *The Nine Lives of Bill Nelson*
1943 *The Dead Look On*
1943 *A Brain and Ten Fingers*
1944 *Faces in a Dusty Picture*

Of the last, a reviewer for the *Times Literary Supplement* noted: "Once more Mr Kersh's specialty is the plain, coarse, lively, everyday speeches of the troops, and again there is much to admire in the vigour and skill of his dialogue and in the assurance with which he draws from it an impression of English character or of English idiosyncracies." Telling dialogue, the manner in which Kersh caught up the usages and rhythms of those about him and in recreating them used them to illuminate caste, milieu and character, was forever his greatest strength. For Kersh, it's not character, but the way in which one uses language, that is fate.

Like birds that never stray over a mile past their birth tree, some writers pass their entire professional lives working the same territory, circling central themes again and again, grinding the meal down ever finer. Others, generally not to their benefit in this ever-increasingly specialized world (for most publishers, booksellers and readers want to be able to say just what kind of sausage it is they are buying), are all over the place. Beginning with *Night and the City*, a mystery novel in the American vein unlike any other written before, and with a firm reputation for war books, Kersh went on to turn out *Prelude to a Certain Midnight*, a mystery novel unlike any other written before or since, before going on to produce intense psychological portraits (*The Thousand Deaths of Mr. Small*), masculine fiction in the Hemingway mold (*The Weak and the Strong*), Huxleyian satire (*An Ape, a Dog and a Serpent*), pulp science fiction (*The Great Wash*, in the U.S. *The Secret Masters*), an outstanding historical novel about Saul's conversion (*The Implacable Hunter*), and demotic, Dickensian comedies (*Fowler's End*).

"I'm sorry, sir, it's just not done that way," British bureaucrats and clerks will tell you when you fail to follow form. And so publishers must have said something of the sort to Gerald Kersh; certainly reviewers said it of him. A general, progressive shrinking of literary boundaries was taking place at the time, a kind of degentrification of the profession. The writer could no longer hope to have it all, to be all things to all men, to write across borders; he was expected to settle down at home and cultivate his garden. He must, to start with, for instance, be either a serious writer or a commercial one.

Kersh, like many of us since, failed to see or admit the distinction.

But surely one did not sit down to write a mystery novel and instead stock it with such darting, solid characters as, in a kind of gentle mutiny, to take over the book entirely? And (as if that were not enough) why on earth or in heaven should one choose to employ with great care all the traditional forms of the genre to the express purpose of calling into question the very meaning and significances of that genre? (Care for a game of tennis? But first, let's have these nets down ...)

Observed from afar, Kersh's career indeed might be seen as one long careen from genre to genre, each shelter in turn blown over by high winds. I've used the word facility above. And I wonder if that, with the changing role of the writer, is not another key on the chain.

Someone said of singer George Jones that it all came too easy to him, that distinctive sound, the phrasing, song interpretation. What others had to work to develop and achieve, he had at his fingertips. Something of the same might be said of Gerald Kersh. Kersh had

160

from the first a terrible facility. He could do anything, it seemed: bring characters to life with one quick phrase, open up their hearts to our view with what they said or avoided saying to one another, show the pettiness, cruelty and wayward kindness aswarm in the anthills of each of us. He could write beautifully, in ways that all but stopped the reader's breath. And he could write knowingly—he was, after all, a soldier—of true ugliness, real horror, of despair that has no past, no future.

Kersh was also a writer of great energy and ambition. Paul Duncan tells us that he often worked night and day with only a couple of hours of sleep, and that eventually this took its toll in regular collapses. One suspects that as time went on Kersh may have leaned a bit heavily on both that energy and on his native facility, expecting them to carry him. "Abundant energy," "exuberance," "imaginative intensity," "pounding creative energy"—these are the sort of phrases one encounters again in contemporary reviews of Kersh's work, just as one encounters, invariably, mention of his prolificacy. And in fact critical opinion seems rather early on to have cast itself and hardened about those notions.

"Just why is Mr. Kersh such an infuriating writer?" the *Sunday Times* asked upon publication of Kersh's collection *Men Without Bones*.

> Because ... we have all been charmed or surprised or shocked at one time or another ... by Mr Kersh's energy and expertness; but with each book there has been less of the writer whose promise we hallooed and more of the casually professional huckster of trinkets and tricks ... There was a time when he looked to have the chance of becoming a Kipling or a Huxley; all we have now is a kind of poor man's Orson Welles of the short story.

Phrases such as "ingenuous and tortuous brilliance" or "a brilliant mess" appear ever more frequently. Anthony Boucher spoke for many, critics as well as readers, in his review of Kersh's effort at a science fiction thriller (*The Secret Masters*):

> The relatively quiet but incisive and suspenseful opening portions of the book are first-rate Kersh, richly peopled with the odd bit roles he sketches so well and written with style and individuality. The large

scale melodrama which develops later is as banal and dated as it is overwritten and incredible.

One of the most thoughful assessments, speaking to Kersh's many strengths as to his weaknesses, came via the *Times Literary Supplement* upon publication of *The Song of a Flea* in 1948.

> Mr. Kersh is at once the delight and despair of his admirers. He is their delight because he is one of the comparatively few living novelists in this country who write with energy and originality and whose ideas are not drawn from a residuum of novels that have been written before; he is their despair because the lack of restraint which makes him such a welcome relief in one direction leads him to all sorts of imperfections in another.

Anthony Burgess, however, rather famously in his 1961 review of *The Implacable Hunter,* took to task the sad and arbitrary state of Kersh's reputation.

> Too many critics affect to mourn a dead talent in Gerald Kersh, a gift that died with his boots clean; there has been a tendency to ignore or disparage his later work, patronise, sigh, and pretend to nostalgia for the tremendous Nelson.

> I can't see why. I read *Fowler's End* in darkest Borneo, at a time when it was hard to laugh, and considered it to be one of the best comic novels of the century, with Sam Yudenow as superb a creation (almost) as Falstaff.

> Many total and partial rereadings have strengthened this conviction. We may adjudge Mr. Kersh, after reading *The Implacable Hunter,* to be now at the height of his powers.

It's impossible to say to what degree Kersh's difficulties in later years were in fact precipitated by changing literary tides, to what degree by editorial preconceptions regarding his work and resistance to it on the part of American publishers, to what degree by his egoism and stubborn insistence upon doing things his way. We know, at any rate, from Paul's biographical sketches, that Kersh had a hard time of it.

Some artists thrive on instability. Hemingway, it was said, required a new woman for each new novel. Others set themselves intricate emotional traps in order to fuel their work. Kersh, instability seems slowly, though progressively, to have undone. To the ever-present fault lines and uncertainties of the freelance life, to market changes and a general decline in the professional's position within publishing, have to be adduced, first, Kersh's failure of health, then a horrendously debilitating marriage, his spendthrift nature, a long series of financial setbacks and unrecoupable losses. It was not that Kersh ever stopped writing. *Fowler's End* came out in 1957, when his problems were well underway, *The Implacable Hunter* in 1961. New stories tumbled from him. But fewer and fewer choices remained open. Profligate with his talents from the first, now he sensed their squander. With books such as *The Great Wash* and *A Long Cool Day in Hell* he was casting about for firm ground, any firm ground.

For me, "The Queen of Pig Island" will always be a central story in Kersh's work. This tale of Lalouette, born without arms and legs, and of Gargantua the Horror who cares for her and of Tick and Tack the Tiny Twins, all of them shipwrecked on an island, manages to compress into just over a dozen pages everything that our civilization and our being human entails. "The Queen of Pig Island" is about love, about treachery, about what society is in its deepest heart and about what men choose to be in theirs. I wonder sometimes if in his final months Gerald Kersh might not have thought back to this story, thought again of Lalouette stranded there so far from the civilization she loved, Lalouette who on that island witnessed the worst and best of which her fellow men were capable, Lalouette arduously, painstakingly scratching on paper with the pencil held in her teeth, working to make a record, to get it all down in the last minutes before, forsaken and utterly alone, she dies.

Charles Willeford
Introduction to
The Black Mass of Brother Springer
Wit's End Publishing
"The World as Willeford and Idea"
by James Sallis

Great writing, my old friend Gene Wolfe says, lies not in doing something better than someone else, but in doing something that no one else can do at all.

Nailed in place for some weeks now while recovering from surgery, I've had the rare blessing of unbridled reading and, with this introduction promised, spent those weeks reading and rereading, with nary an excuse in sight, the works of Charles Willeford, who seems to me the very exemplar of what Gene meant.

No one writes like Willeford. In much the same way as Jim Thompson and David Goodis, he was able to take advantage of a window of opportunity that existed in the Fifties and hitch a ride on the mile-long train of original paperback novels. Turning in product that seemed to conform, these writers in fact produced books largely sui generis, books deeply stained with the personalities of their authors, like the indelible grime beneath a mechanic's fingernails. "I had a hunch that madness was the predominant theme and normal condition for Americans in the second half of the century," Willeford once said, a madness that spilled into every word he wrote, from the sinister car salesman of *High Priest of California* to *Miami Blues'* Freddy Frenger and *Sideswipe's* Troy Louden. The normal condition. Reading Willeford's work in bulk, as I have done these past weeks, can be like attending a family reunion of Lou Fords, walking into a roomful of Ripleys.

It's with Chester Himes, I think, that Willeford best compares; they seem at times two sides of a single coin. Both were literary writers whose tales of obsessed individuals fascinate as much as they repulse. Both, willfully, wrote from society's narrowest outside edge, each phrase and scene saturated with a sense of the absurd, of suffering, of the many ways in which society twists its people into monsters and the many ways in which they visit violence back upon that society. In Himes and Willeford, savagery and comedy are forever bedmates. They do not subvert the genre so much as they defy it: Don't hold back, baby, show me what you can do, show me what you have.

As I wrote in my book *Difficult Lives,* I believe that popular fiction at its best offers a unique portrait of its time. It sends tendrils down to the very baserock of what we are as a nation and who we are as individuals, shines a light into corners where crouch our deepest fears, unvoiced assumptions, basest aspirations. *The Invasion of the Body Snatchers* tells us far more about cold-war paranoia and the American dream as lived in the Fifties than any shelf full of sociology texts.

The Black Mass of Brother Springer appeared in 1958, Willeford's fourth published novel. *High Priest of California*, 1953, had seen print as half of a Royal Giant, bound with Talbot Mundy's adventure novel *Full Moon.* Willeford wrote it while stationed at Hamilton Air Force Base; weekends, he'd drive down to San Francisco, check into the Powell Hotel, and spend both days writing. Its tale of used car salesman Russell Haxby introduced the kind of amoral protagonist that was to become a Willeford trademark. In 1955 Beacon Books, like Royal a wing of Universal Publishing and Distributing, brought out *Pick-Up*, with its tale of a failed painter and the woman who, walking into the diner where he works as short-order cook, changes his life. A year later Beacon issued Willeford's third novel, *Wild Wives*, double-bound with a reprint of *High Priest.*

When *Black Mass* came out, Willeford was thirty-nine years old, two years retired after twenty years' service in the Army and Air Force. If

Cockfighter, as many believe, is Willeford's purest existentialist novel, one to be taken at the level of Horace McCoy's *They Shoot Horses Don't They* and Albert Camus' *L'Etranger*—and this is arguably the case—then *Black Mass* is a close second, its double: another *monstre délicat,* its *semblable,* its *frère.* For the existentialist, consciousness, the very core of our being, is an emptiness waiting to be filled by arbitrary choices. We must practice faith in the absence of belief. We become ourselves through our actions.

The Black Mass of Brother Springer was Willeford's original title, one which Universal, more comfortable with titles on the order of *Hitch-Hike Hussy,* quickly rejected. The publisher also rejected Willeford's tongue-in-cheek suggestion for an alternative title, *Nigger Lover,* bringing the book out as *Honey Gal.* An entry in the author's diary for September 1957 states that Bob Abramson of Universal Publishing bought the novel for $250 on acceptance and $250 on publication, "a hell of a low price for six weeks of hard work."

Briefly, the novel tells the story of a stalled writer who, desperately trolling for a story, meets a retired Army sergeant who has taken over the Church of God's Flock in a kind of preemptive strike and now is about to jump ship. First, though, he ordains Sam Springer and sends him off to Jax to serve as pastor of an all-black church. There, Brother Springer becomes entangled in the civil rights movement, including a proposed boycott of city services.

> On my part, I had no personal motives, nothing to gain one way or another. I didn't believe in what I was doing, and I didn't disbelieve in it either. I was indifferent. But the plan was interesting, almost exciting, and I wanted to see how it would work out.

The novel is replete with typically marvelous bits of description ("The outside of the chicken was a beautiful color—the shade of a two-day bruise on the tender side of a woman's thigh") and typically Willefordian slyness (during Brother Springer's initial sermon, on Kafka, he muses: "And I was trying to make them think! How unfair of me, how unlike a minister of the gospel!").

Beware enterprises that require new clothes, Emerson warned. Willeford is seldom funnier than when writing about clothes (Hoke Moseley's yellow jumpsuits come to mind), and each of Springer's transmogrifications is heralded by new clothing. When, after selling his novel, he goes to his workplace to resign, he dresses in

> a pair of leather sandals, a pair of red linen slacks, a pale yellow sport shirt imprinted with tiny red rickshaws, and a white linen jacket. I placed dark sunglasses over my nose, and a straw hat with a solid yellow band upon my head. These clothes had been purchased several weeks before and had been put aside for the occasion.

On the bus to Jax, now become Brother Sam Deuteronomy Springer, he muses on the puissance of his ill-fitting dark twill suit.

> As the Abbott had implied, clerical garb made the minister; I had not been given any other instructions to go with the uniform. The mere donning of my black suit changed me, not only in the eyes of the world, but in my own eyes.

And near book's end, following his apostasy:

> We looked through racks until I found a suit that I wanted. The material was thin, a mixture of dacron, nylon and polished Egyptian cotton. The color was a glistening tint of powder blue, matching my eyes exactly. The jacket, without shoulder padding, hugged my round shoulders perfectly ...
>
> In less than an hour I was a new man, if clothes do make the man. To go with my blue suit I had purchased a Hathaway button-down shirt with tiny blue-and-red checks. A knitted maroon tie looked well with the shirt, and to match the tie I had chosen a pair of all-wool maroon socks. Broad-winged cordovan shoes and a chestnut Tyrolean hat with a gay yellow feather in the band completed my outfit.

As Marshall Jon Fisher pointed out in a piece for *the Atlantic* a few years back, Sam Springer is "a characteristically Willefordian amalgam of selfish mercenary and well-meaning drifter," careening through life with little thought for the future, borne from one moment's need, one moment's chance opportunity, to the next. He became a writer as capriciously as he becomes a reverend, he leaves his wife with hardly a moment's regret or serious consideration, he sheds the old skin and slithers away.

In some regards, of course, America is a land with no past or future, only an eternal present, and Willeford's work is filled with characters looking to start over, as though continual reinvention were the very juice and squeezed pulp of the American experience: Hoke Moseley in his return to Singer Island, Troy Louden with his one big score before retiring to Haiti, Frank Mansfield whose life will end (and begin again?) once he wins Cockfighter of the Year.

It's a wonderful, defining moment when late in the novel ex-sergeant Abbott Dover returns to tell Brother Springer that he made a mistake in ordaining him, to admit that he's read Springer's novel, and to thank Springer for making it possible for him to find love. Of the boycott he asks:

> "But do you care? Does it make any difference to you, Springer, one way or the other?"
>
> "No. Not really." I didn't lie to Dover. His flat blue eyes with their frank and piercing stare demanded the truth and nothing else.
>
> "I found that out when I read your novel. A clever little book. Why not? You're a well-read man, and the characters said brittle and clever things, the surface brilliance of a thousand books you've read, and not an original idea of your own on a single page. Cute situations, complications in the right places, and the inevitable straight romantic plot with the obvious ending. You don't know a damned thing about people, and even less about yourself."

That the novel bears indelibly the mark of its creator, all of that creator's bright and dark, was something Willeford believed deeply; it is also something that, reading him, we come to believe. If popular fiction is the secret and true history of its time, so can the novel at its best become the inmost record of self. In an essay from 1953, published thirty-five years later in Mystery Scene and reprinted in *Writing & Other Blood Sports* (Dennis McMillan Publications), Charles Willeford addresses the creative process:

> The novel is a case history of the writer. It is the story of his life written as well as he can write it. It never ends; it goes on

day after day, year after year. He is his own hero, his own heroine, his villain, his minor characters—the thoughts of each of these are his own thoughts twisting and churning and wrenched alive and crawling from his conscious and unconscious mind. He writes because he must, because to fail as a writer means to fail as a man ...

When I first began to write it was an act of desperation. It was a blind search, and at first every trail I followed led to the inside of a deep cave. I was searching with my conscious mind instead of my heart ...

I lost all hope; I reached the point where I no longer cared what people thought about my writing. And that is when I began to write....

I scrapped all of my early efforts and started over again. I put my feelings, my heart, my life, my innermost thoughts on paper.

That, my friends, whether that art comes wrapped in lurid, waxy covers or swaddled in the imprimatur of prestigious publishers, is high art.

Following the Civil War, pawn shops were filled with brass instruments left over from military bands. Dirt cheap, they were taken up by black musicians, many of them ex-slaves, who on these instruments searched for and created a new music, a specifically American music, jazz. So too with writers such as Chester Himes, Jim Thompson and Charles Willeford. They took up a form poorly suited perhaps to the measure of their vision and by sheer force of personality, by will and brute creativity, bent the form to their end, bringing into the world a music never heard before, a new and enduring art.

Shirley Jackson
For *The Magazine of Fantasy & Science Fiction*
Shirley Jackson: A Rather Haunted Life, by Ruth Franklin, 2016,
Liveright Publishing Corporation/W.W. Norton & Company, $35.00.
"On Shirley Jackson"
  by James Sallis

For four days the ground moved.
This from real life, from a man giving witness to mass executions
in his village during WWII, with entire families lined up and shot,
to fall forward into trenches dead or nearly so and be covered over.

There's more terror in that brief sentence and its accompanying
image than in a thousand drooling monsters. What does it have to
do with Shirley Jackson? Horror builds from what you sense yet don't
see, things moving beneath the surface, dark shapes at the corner of
mind and vision. And with that, you're in Shirley Jackson land.

Shirley Jackson: A Rather Haunted Life is the second major
biography, following upon 1988's *Private Demons: The Life of
Shirley Jackson* by Judy Oppenheimer and two collections of
miscellany, *Just an Ordinary Day* (1995) and *Let Me Tell You* (2015).
In 2010 Jackson's work joined The Library of America in a volume
edited by Joyce Carol Oates: 800-plus pages, two classic novels *The
Haunting of Hill House* and *We Have Always Lived in the Castle*,
46 stories and sketches. Perhaps all this will collude to bring the
focused attention Shirley Jackson has long deserved.

Or maybe not. Maybe in the public mind she'll continue to be known only as author of "The Lottery." Ruth Franklin's introduction to this outstanding biography touches on some of the reasons recognition has been so long delayed. Jackson wrote, she says, always with a central interest in women's lives, and in genres regarded as "faintly disreputable," turning plots and characters on a lathe so distinctly personal as to produce a body of work that's finally uncategorizable. And since there's no ready drawer for what Jackson wrote, all too often it gets cut down to fit. *The Haunting of Hill House* is received as simply a well written ghost story, *We Have Always Lived in the Castle* as a standard mystery. Meanwhile, what is to be made of those lightly comic tales of suburban life with the kids? How on earth do those fit in?

It's all a confusion, all a tangle.

As was Shirley Jackson's life.

She was, from the first, resolutely a commercial writer. Even while essaying the problem of evil, as in "One Ordinary Day with Peanuts," she anchored her work in the domestic, so that the stories have about them an easy familiarity, an apparent lightness in sharp contrast to the chasms and gorges beneath.

"No writer since Henry James has been so successful in exploring the psychological reach of terror," Franklin writes.

And Shirley Jackson herself: "I have always loved to use fear, to take it and comprehend it and make it work."

● ● ●

My name is Mary Katherine Blackwood. I am eighteen years old, and I live with my sister Constance. I have often thought that with any luck at all I could have been born a werewolf, because the two middle fingers on both my hands are the same length, but I have had to be content with what I had. I dislike washing myself, and dogs, and noise. I like my sister Constance, and Richard Plantagenet, and Amanita phalloides, the death-cup mushroom. Everyone else in my family is dead.
We Have Always Lived in the Castle

● ● ●

Plenty of fear to work with, plenty of contrast, an abundance of tamped-down pain, all of which grew as years wore on.

She wrote in quick bites, hours seized here and there—stories for *The New Yorker*, dozens of vignettes and stories for *Saturday Evening Post*, *Mademoiselle*, and *Good Housekeeping*, six novels—while raising four children, maintaining some semblance of a normal suburban household, pursuing an active social life with husband Stanley Edgar Hyman, and hiding out from neighbors estranged by the family's oddness, all this as she struggled upstream of a crushing sense of failure and fragility, prolonged bouts of depression, and occasional hospitalizations.

That sentence may give you some idea of the tangle of her life. All told, she was out there pitching for 24 years, dying of heart failure in 1965 aged 48. From 1961 on, she was essentially housebound.

Her second novel, *Hangsaman* (1951), recounts the emotional breakdown of a young woman fleeing her poisonous homelife for an ever stronger fantasy world overseen by the imaginary Tony, an amalgam of the protagonist's own anxiety and turmoil.

In *The Bird's Nest* (1954, filmed as *Lizzie*) Elizabeth Richmond, a woman with multiple personalities, one day arrives at work in the town's museum to find that the wall of her office has been removed and that she can extend her arm into the gaping hole, into nothingness. As again and again, a building is central to the tale; the dissolution of the building and of Elizabeth are one and the same. Already she is so fractured, so insubstantial, that coworkers barely register her presence. Franklin praises scenes in which Elizabeth sets out four coffee cups, one for each personality, and another in which Elizabeth watches as each personality in turn takes a bath.

The Sundial (1958, four years after the first hydrogen bomb test) was Jackson's own favorite of her novels. Behind the walls of the Halloran estate, built by a businessman who "could think of nothing better to do with his money than set up his own world," the profoundly broken Halloran family gathers to await apocalypse, after which they will, as deserved, come forth into "a world clean and silent."

Centering on another dissolution, *The Haunting of Hill House* (1959, filmed at least twice) may very well be the best ghost story ever written. It *is* a ghost story, but above all it's the story of a woman's steady erasure from forces within and without in a world where longing and dread, what is most feared and most hoped for, speak the same language. A ghost story, yes—but one as much aligned with Flannery O'Connor, Patricia Highsmith, Faulkner, and Camus as with any standard fare.

> With what she perceived as quick cleverness she pressed her foot down hard on the accelerator … I can hear them calling now, she thought, and the little footsteps running through Hill House and the soft sound of the hills pressing closer … I am really doing it, she thought …
> In the unending, crashing second before the car hurled into the tree she thought clearly, Why am I doing this? Why am I doing this? Why don't they stop me?

Three years after *Hill House* came *We Have Always Lived in the Castle* with its tale of two sisters shunned by their community for the presumed murder of their family. In those first lines—*My name is Mary Katherine Blackwood. I am eighteen years old, and I live with my sister Constance … Everyone else in my family is dead*—the narrator leans close to say she has something important to tell you, and though you trust none of what she says and know that listening may lead you to terrible places, you do listen, and you follow. *We Have Always Lived in the Castle* is utterly original, a feast for readers, a how-to manual for writers. It would be the last novel.

• • •

In 1958, while working on *Hill House*, Jackson wrote a letter to her husband, calling out his indifference to her and the children, his retreat into work and the attention of his female students, her own loneliness, his affairs with other women. She ends by reminding him that he once wrote a letter to her to say she would never be lonely again, that this was the first and most dreadful lie he ever told her.

Just as the house of Usher in its collapse memorialized the passing of the Old South and a once grand, now degraded style of living, *Hill House* echoes the crumbling of Shirley's marriage, or of her belief in it. Nothing can ever again be as it once seemed. Eleanor believes the house in its haunting has called to her, inviting her to become one with it. *I am home, I am home*, she thinks, not long before driving her car into a tree.

In both the last novels Jackson's art is at a very high level indeed. But sadly, as Franklin writes, "the trajectory of Jackson's creative ascent was mirrored by an arc of personal descent." The depression that had been a lifelong companion, the predative feelings of rejection and helplessness, crowded ever closer, exacerbated perhaps by drinking and by the amphetamines she'd taken for years for weight control. Obese, in poor general health, hamstrung by feelings of betrayal, she was unable to write, barely able to leave the house and to cope with details of everyday life.

She was on her way back up and again writing—three new stories, a piece for the Saturday Evening Post, 75 pages of a new novel, *Come Along with Me*—when on an August afternoon in 1965 her husband came to wake her from a nap and could not.

● ● ●

Shirley Jackson: A Rather Haunted Life is an artful, elegant book that does honor to its subject. Ruth Franklin writes extraordinarily well, with fine narrative instincts. She keeps things moving, never allowing the story to founder (as do so many biographies) in facts and details or be strangled by its timeline, forever aware that she is indeed telling a *story*, often stepping briefly forward and back to suggest connections that flower as we read on. We clearly sense the ranging of Franklin's mind across the ciphers and crosses of Jackson's life and, behind that, the ranging of Jackson's own, both of them trying to make sense of the pieces. It's a biography that wears its surmise lightly in much the way that accomplished fiction does, knowing the pieces cannot fit together snugly but nudging at them, moving them about again and again, trying for the best fit possible.

Shirley Jackson used to take the kids out onto the porch during storms and howl back at the thunder. "The very nicest thing about being a writer," she wrote in one essay, "is that you can afford to indulge yourself endlessly with oddness, and nobody can really do anything about it, as long as you keep writing and kind of using it up." One finishes this biography with full gratitude for all that Shirley Jackson's "using it up" has given us.

Truly amazing, what can come of howling back at the thunder.